How to Be a Better Dude and Treat Your Lady Right

Your Ultimate Study-Guide for Transforming Yourself

Around the World, Women are Enjoying the Experience of Their New, Transformed Man.

This study-guide book was written for men who are looking for real answers! It is STRICTLY for those men who are ready to improve how they interact with their most Precious Lady:

- Either because they recognize that they are about to blow it and lose the most important person in their life!

- Or, they want major self-improvement on who they are and want to increase the quality of their man-woman relationship.

You'll Get: 156 - page study guide – **6** FREE audio recordings which are seven to ten minutes in length – Plus an additional FREE Bonus Gift of One **New Man Mind Training** Audio for rapid, high impact, and long-term self-improvement.

Get ready because it hits you hard and fast. I will say to you what she won't say, or she is too afraid to say.

**Gentlemen, I speak the way that reality says that it is.
I tell you the TRUTH, and I Hope You Can Handle It!**

You Are The Love Of My Life!

How to Be a Better Dude and Treat Your Lady Right

To Enhance Your Learning FREE Audio Downloads for You!

Please listen to them in the order listed below.

They are seven to ten minutes in length. These audios are helpful in providing you with greater insight for some of the key lessons of the study-guide book.

> Introduction - **Purpose of this Study-Guide Book**
> Brain Science - **Why Does This Work**
> Audio #1 - **It's Decision Time**
> Audio #2 - **Learning How to Say I'm Sorry**
> Audio #3 - **Bad Attitude Dude**
> Insight - **Look into the Mirror**
> *** **New Man Mind Trainer Audio – 30 minutes**

> When you are listening to the New Man Mind Audio it is best to use ear-plugs or headphones.

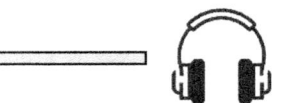

Desktop/Laptop: for best viewing use this link --- Click Here for Access
 * Or just type in - desktop.howtobeabetterdude.com

Mobile Device: for best viewing use this link ------ Click Here for Access
 * Or just type in - mobile.howtobeabetterdude.com

Tablet Device: for best viewing use this link ------ Click here for Access
 * Or just type in - tablet.howtobeabetterdude.com

Special Note: The last audio is your most important. This is your New Man Mind Trainer Audio. Recommended listening is at least 5 days per week. However, the more you listen, the better. Typically, you should notice a real difference within yourself in about 4 to 6 weeks depending on your frequency and consistency of use.

You will need 30 minutes of quiet time to listen to this audio. It has high impact and enhances the development of new thoughts, ideas, and actions towards your Precious Lady. Brain Entrainment Technology is encoded into the deep, relaxing background music so that the message is more easily captured and retained by your brain.

Download Instructions:

- Click on the link for access to all of the audios.
- **Download each of the seven (7) audios.**
- Sign up for Our Epic Weekly Blog updates.
- You can unsubscribe from the blog at any time.
- Got stuck or have a question email me at:

   Jeff@HowToBeABetterDude.com

How to Be a Better Dude and Treat Your Lady Right

How to know if you could benefit from this study-guide book?

Please understand that there is no condemnation in being truthful about your answers. My steadfast confession to you throughout this entire study-guide book is that many years ago, I had massively corrupted mental operating programs that clouded my thinking and ruled my actions.

I was GUILTY of answering any, and all of these questions with a BIG **FAT** YES! No, I was never proud of the old me, but in order to correct the problems within me, I HAD to be honest with myself no matter how terrible, creepy and regretful I may have felt. The Great Awakening Had Begun!

This journey is one of heightened self-awareness and far-reaching self-discovery; so, it is imperative that you are honest with yourself and know exactly where you are right now as you begin your transformation.

These questions are straight-forward. They help you to become more aware of your negative thoughts, words, and actions towards the Love of Your Life.

- Do you get angry easily at your partner or anyone else?
- Do little things frustrate you or irritate you?
- Do you have ready-to-go hair trigger irritability?
- Do you ever belittle the ideas or thoughts of your lady?
- Has your lady asked you to stop hurting her, and you still do so?
- Do you exhibit a short attention span when your lady is speaking?
- Would you say that you yell, scream and curse at your precious lady?
- Do you demean or degrade your lovely lady?
- Do you verbally abuse your special lady in ANY way?
- Do you call your precious love bad or harsh names?
- Do you threaten, tease, bully and intimidate your lady in ANY way?
- Do you get angry with other situations in life, and take it out on her?
- Are you for no reason moody, grumpy or just pissed off at times?
- If things go wrong outside of your relationship, do you blame your lady?
- Do you display anger on the road while driving your car?
- Do you get angry at inanimate objects and burst out swearing?
- Do you just blurt out swear words when things aren't right?
- Are you impatient or easily irritated by the actions of others?
- When grumpy and moody, do you speak rudely to your lady?
- Do you use a sharp, snappy tone of speech with you lovely lady?
- Do you reject and resent help or assistance from your precious lady?
- Do you have a snappy fast-moving tongue and wrong drawn conclusions?
- Do you display rapid, instant out of the blue irritability with your lady?

"My Beautiful Lady is a Heaven-Sent Gift & I Thank My God in Heaven for Her"

How to Be a Better Dude and Treat Your Lady Right

Table of Contents

Insight I Epic Life Changing Results – What can this do for you?
Insight II Re-wire Your Brain and Become a Better Dude
Insight III Decision and Your Power to Choose. Choose Wisely!
Insight IV The Truth Be Told – Bold Upfront and in Your Face
Insight V Mission and Vision Statement
Insight VI Wake Up and Become Self-Aware of Your Thoughts
Insight VII You Must Be Willing to Improve Your Thoughts & Actions
Insight VIII Repeated Use Improves What You Think and How You Act
Insight IX Proactive and Save Your Relationship
Insight X How to Become a Better Dude Transformation Process
Insight Letter * Special Insight from the Author

Chapter 1 - page 1….. **The Truth Exposed – We are all programmed**
    You may not like what I say, but it is the truth!

Chapter 2 - page 5….. **Brain Science Insight**
    A detailed look at how your thoughts develop in your brain.

Chapter 3 - page 12…. **You Choose How You Want to Be**
    Yes, you have a choice in how you will treat your Precious Lady!

Chapter 4 - page 17…. **How Did We Get So Jacked-Up in the First Place?**
    The life-long programming of our brains for relationship failure.

Chapter 5 - page 28…. Special Report
    Music, radio, and television ARE driving your thoughts… believe it, bro!

Chapter 6 - page 32…. **Over 21 yrs. Chronologically, but Acting 10 yrs. Emotionally**
    So, you THINK that you are a man? Well, read this! You won't like it!

Chapter 7 - page 38…. **Are You Guilty of Destroying Her Emotionally?**
    If this is you, then you should be truly ashamed of your actions!

Chapter 8 - page 49…. **Loves Potent Killers – Ignore & Neglect**
    This is ripping her to pieces and crushing her mentally!

Chapter 9 - page 54…. **No Physical Affection for Your Lady from You!**
    Inexcusable and deplorable physical inactions by you that destroy her!

Chapter 10 page 60…. **Beer, The Boys and Leaving Her Alone, Again.**
    Such a jerk! The best thing in your life and you are blowing it!

How to Be a Better Dude and Treat Your Lady Right

<u>Chapter 11</u> - page 65…. **Bad Attitude Dude – Mean, grumpy & moody men**
                              Are you acting like a mean, rotten low-life towards her? Why?

<u>Chapter 12</u> - page 78…. **Men, Let the Healing Begin**
                              Learning the Art of Saying the words, "I am Sorry"

<u>Chapter 13</u> - page 85…. **Breaking the Cycle of Negative Thoughts & Words Spoken**
            page 87…… * The Power of Using Conscious Compensating Controls
            page 93…… * Washing Your Brain of the Old While Learning the New

<u>Chapter 14</u> - page 95…. **Most Powerful Secret Language on Earth**
                              Start to learn this to communicate to her heart

<u>Chapter 15</u> - page 106… **Actions that Start Communicating to Her Heart**
                              Your new mind training plan to win her heart, again

<u>Review 15</u> - page 117… **Special Chapter 15 Wrap-up**
                              Why should you master Chapter 15?

<u>Chapter 16</u> - page 118… **A Better Way to Communicate – No More Excuses**
                              How to avoid stupid, unproductive communications

<u>Chapter 17</u> - page 127… **Words & Actions Together Is Love's Secret Language**
                              Sample actions, words, phrases and statements to implement

<u>Chapter 18</u> - page 133… **Design Your Every Day**
                              Put together a vision for how you want your day to go

<u>Insight</u>   - page 138… **Personal Growth & Your Transformation**

<u>The Closing</u> - page 139 …**Your Decision and the Power of Choice**

<u>Brain Training Instruction Sheet</u>

Subscribe to Our Epic Blog for Becoming a Better Dude
http://blogsignup.howtobeabetterdude.com

How to Be a Better Dude and Treat Your Lady Right

Epic Life-Changing Results

How to Treat Her Better…
- Stop her bleeding heart
- Stop the emotional abuse
- Stop the yelling and cursing
- Stop the anger and rage
- Stop the mental torment
- Stop the degrading, cruel words
- Stop your caustic and toxic tongue

Discover How To…
- Apologize in the best of ways
- Heal her broken heart
- Become self-aware of your thoughts
- Become a new and better man
- Treat her better and right every day
- <u>Re-wire your brain for love success</u>
- Think good, speak good and do good
- Repair the damage that you have created

Becoming the Master of Your Thoughts, You CAN…
- Eliminate harmful negative thoughts
- Improve the image you have of yourself
- Acquire new enriching, positive thoughts
- Become a Better Man for your lady
- Stop being mean & grumpy towards her
- Stop cursing and swearing at your lady
- Be the man who builds her up

Get Rid of Lies About Yourself…
- That you could never change
- You are just the way that you are
- You can't change your personality
- You just can't stop being this way

Become a Better Man With…
- The quality of your thoughts
- Your actions and your behaviors
- Generating positive thoughts
- Creative displays of love
- Increasing levels of patience

Become More…
- Positive
- Uplifting
- Inspiring
- Empathic
- Caring
- Transparent
- Patient
- Understanding
- Thoughtful
- Loving
- Gentle
- Kind
- Appreciative
- Insightful

Your Enemy to Growth & Change
- #1 enemy to prevent your growth
- Why is your #1 enemy against you
- How to defeat your #1 enemy

Brain Science Helps You Treat Her Better
- Understanding your brain neurons
- Brain neurons help you to grow
- What is a Neural-Network
- Positive Neural Network = Better Love

and so much MORE!

Insight I

Rewire Your Brain to Become a Better Man

The science behind how you can become a "Transformed Man" is not a mysterious or complicated process. In fact, it has been shown to be quite simple and is based on how the brain works naturally. Treating your Precious Lovely Lady with the best of heart at all times, under all conditions is a worthy mission. If you have fallen far short, or you have personality quirks and attitudes that are damaging to her and the relationship — or you are on the brink of losing her — then you CAN change. This study-guide book can lead you to life-changing results when you regularly apply the mental exercises outlined. It is now all up to you and your desire to change, grow and become a better man.

⬇ **New Information**
⬇ **New Thoughts**
⬇ **New Feelings**
⬇ **New Attitudes**
⬇ **New Beliefs**
⬇ **New Speech**
⬇ **New Actions**
⬇ **New Behaviors**
⬇ **New Habits**

A New Man

The 9 steps above are a part of the process to re-wiring your brain to become a New and Better Man. This is how you will eliminate negative, useless, corrupted, insensitive and reckless thoughts, speech, and behaviors. This is how you will create new, permanent, attractive, life-changing positive thoughts, actions, and behaviors that begin to heal the heart of the Love of Your Life and save your highly-treasured relationship with your Precious Lady. No excuses, my friend. It is time to man-up!

Decision and Your Power to Choose

Throughout this entire study-guide book, you will be challenged and pushed to make a **decision**! That **decision** is to change, grow and become more than what you are, or to stay exactly as you are!

The Power to Choose is TOTALLY Within "YOUR" Control

You can "**choose**" to grow and become the man of her dreams. Or, you can keep the old, corrupted, broken and negative ways of being, while she endures the mental anguish and sadness that she relives every day of her life because of your actions.

Yes, the decision that you make with your power to "choose" will either make you or break you and your Precious Lady.

This e-book is straight-forward; it's a "slap-you-in-your-face" approach for the first eight chapters.

However, after a little tough love, I provided you with seven life-changing proactive action steps that you can incorporate into your new way of being. They help you to get on the right track of self-improvement, with the end goal of becoming a "Transformed Man;" a man who knows how to treat his lady and become the man of her dreams, all the time.

None of this will happen if you decide to ignore the lessons contained within this book. You have the power to "choose" a better way. The information shared with you here will allow you to find that way. You must apply the knowledge daily to get the desired results.

My friends, the Power to Choose and the Decisions you make are in YOUR control. It will be the final determination of where your present and future relationships will go to from this day forward.

Choose Wisely!

Make the Right Decision!

She is Worth It!

The Truth Be Told
Proceed with These Words of Caution

If You Are Not Ready to Grow and Change, then you should stop reading this book immediately!

Attention: This book is a high impact relationship book for men who would like to improve the quality of their thoughts, communication, and actions with their Special Lady in life. Upon first reading it, one could get the impression that I am bashing the heck out of the male species! This is 100%, not the case!

However, what I am doing is speaking up and being brutally honest on behalf of the many women who are driven into a state of emotional turmoil and distress. This is all because of your thoughtless and selfish actions!

IF you are ready to make a change in the ways that you relate to your precious and most Special Lady, then this book is perfect for you!

IF you ARE NOT ready to make a change, then please, I strongly encourage you to continue reading anyway. You can at least learn more about how much damage, or potential damage you are likely to cause to your Special Lady if you stay as you are. Also, you will come to understand the enormous mental and emotional strain that your woman lives with, and how you are too blind to realize it!

Do You Truly Love Your Woman? Then fully embrace this study-guide book because it will surely open your eyes and reveal new thought-provoking concepts for you to self-improve as a man. It will begin the process of re-building you and healing your damaged relationship!

For those of you who complete this book and apply the principles of "How to Be a Better Man and Treat Your Lady Right," then your life with your Special Lady will begin to change almost immediately! You can become the man you wanted to be with continued application of the information you now have before your eyes.

Don't Shoot the Messenger!

I'm merely saying what she wants you to know!

How to Be a Better Dude and Treat Your Lady Right

MISSION STATEMENT

> The multi-faceted mission and vision of this study-guide book and audios are to provide you with piercing insight on what you can do to improve yourself and have a healthy, vibrant relationship with the Love of Your Life.
>
> Your actions and reactions may be causing your lady to be fearful of you, or to be withdrawn from you. This information will show you how to correct your short-comings and bring about the healing of your own heart first, and that will translate into healing of the damaged, broken and hardened heart of the lady who you love so deeply.
>
> Overall you will also find that I provide you specialized knowledge for you to implement, which will help you to acquire new attitudes and actions that are positive, healthy and uplifting that women highly desire in a man.

This study-guide book was written to educate and empower men on how to communicate directly with the heart of a woman and connect to where she can believe in you and know that you are TOTALLY INTO HER! *Scary, huh?*

Within this information, you will find that I pull out all the stops! I was upfront with you when I stated that if you have any reservations about performing the actions that were suggested or performing the recommended behavioral adjustments, then **YOU WILL SURELY FAIL** on winning back the heart of that Special Lady!

If you choose the path that leads to failure, and you become sick to your stomach and miserable because you have lost that best thing that has ever happened to you, then go and look into the mirror and ask this question, ***"Why did this happen?"***

The answer will come to you quickly because the answer will be what is reflecting in the mirror! **YOU!!!**

Disclaimer: **The methods and information for improved communications in this book ARE NOT a 100% fix for all relationship problems. Sometimes, we as men, have treated the most Precious Lady in our world so poorly, that it is beyond the repair of natural intervention. Therefore, can only be healed with the Supernatural Intervention of God Himself!**

Wake Up and Become Self-Aware of Your Thoughts

The major problem with some of us (guys), when we are angry or frustrated, is that we move our big mouths too quickly to speak words. Many times, we do this spontaneously, and we do it without regard to how hurtful or damaging it may be.

Yes, we have done this kind of action so many times that we have become experts at delivering these scornful remarks with the express intent to verbally brutalize, with the primary objective being to purposefully scar, bruise and emotionally damage our Precious Lady.

As of today, you hopefully will "CHOOSE" a new way of being! It all starts with becoming self-aware with nearly every thought that enters your head. Then, filter it out if it is negative, ugly or mean BEFORE you open your mouth.

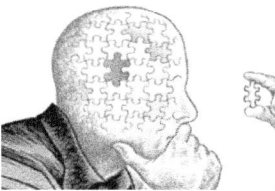

Your thoughts are the force behind ALL of your actions, behaviors, and habits! It is your thoughts that are driving you to treat your lady in such a sub-standard manner. It is your thoughts that you must get better at managing and work to improve.

Personally, my thoughts <u>were</u> extremely toxic, and full of massive amounts of negative energy, especially towards my girlfriends years ago. This was in part due to what I had learned from others who had gone before. These men were figures of authority to me, and they were my examples in life on how to "handle" a woman. However, once I became <u>Consciously Aware</u> of my thoughts, I dramatically improved on what I spoke, and how I acted.

To save your relationship and to take yourself to a whole new level of being, you MUST gain insight into your thoughts. In this study guide, you will learn how to do this, and then learn, how to modify them at the Speed of Your Thoughts. When you do so, you are physically re-wiring your brain, which improves your thoughts, your actions, and your behaviors! And eventually, New Positive Habits are Born!

The Great Awakening is When You Become Self-Aware of Your Thoughts.

You MUST Be Willing to Improve Your Thoughts and Your Actions!

The information contained in this study-guide book will work if your desire to grow and change certain aspects of yourself is strong! Meanwhile, you must follow the various mental exercises outlined. By moving forward with "How to Be a Better Dude and Treat Your Lady Right," you significantly increase your chances of returning the trust, love and beautiful future together with the Love of Your Life.

Critical Note: **To make this work, you MUST be on fire with a white-hot desire to self-improve in the art of communication and giving yourself selflessly to that Special Lady every day!**

The choice is within the scope of your power! It is not difficult, IF… you truly want to change! Women want to be loved. They also want a man that can effectively communicate that love in a multitude of ways that move them to the very core of their being!

If you have recently lost your lady or the relationship is on shaky ground; let's be hopeful that all is not lost!

You can turn it around, but ONLY if you act and continue to follow up with positive actions that build a path to the heart of that Special Lady!

Men, we **MUST stop being unconscious** to the needs of women! We are blind to the fact of how they were acting, and what they had been saying until it is too late!!!

It is time to stop focusing on your penis and its immediate urgencies, and to focus thoroughly and intensely on the heart and mind of your Lovely Lady!

Don't get me wrong; the whole sex thing is vitally important, but when you eliminate making love to the heart, mind, spirit, and soul of the woman, you will lose that relationship! The flames of love will eventually fade if you don't mentally and emotionally treat right.

I strongly encourage you to make a commitment to work through this study guide, and the highly-recommended suggestions provided for producing a beautiful and dynamic love relationship with the Love of Your Life.

Insight VII

How to Be a Better Dude and Treat Your Lady Right

This Information Fully Embraced and Applied is Life-Changing! Repeated Use Improves "What" You Think and "How" You Act.

Great News! The vast majority of relationships CAN be helped and healed, just by you being thoughtful and considerate on how you speak to your Lovely Lady. However, it is like anything else in the world of self-improvement, <u>you must be willing to practice, drill, rehearse and embrace the words and actions with deep-seated emotion at the core of your being!</u>

Yep, you have to learn how to speak of your FEELINGS in a sincere, warm heart-felt way! Another way of saying it is that you must learn how to spill your guts with NO FEAR!!

How long before you can see results from your new mode of being?

It varies, based on a number of factors; such as length of relationship, the strength of the relationship, how long you have been lacking in communicating with her heart, and the level of energy you put forth into this restoration and healing process!

For many, it starts to happen within a matter of a few days, IF YOU ARE REAL!

<u>Note:</u> IF you have been the kind of man who has been cruel, insensitive, insulting and one who belittles, criticizes, condemns, and repetitively destroys her emotionally by screaming, yelling and swearing at her, DO NOT expect her to believe you at first when you claim that you have changed!

You must become a reformed man, and reformation takes time. It begins to show itself in small ways! However, stay patient and consistent with your new attitude of being a gentle-spirit of with mindset positive expectation in all that you do.

> ## This is not to be taken and implemented as some quick fix, microwaveable, superficial, phony-baloney action plan!

Guys, I am talking about you flushing out the junk of how you used to be! You will learn how to think at a higher level and correct unwanted negative behavior traits.

Insight VIII

Be Proactive and Save The Love of Your Life!

Unfortunately, for many, you will blow this life-changing information off. You will end up losing the most precious and coveted gift of your entire life; your soulmate! If this does happen to you, then it will be your haunting lesson in love for the rest of your days on this earth!

All because your ego and pride got in your way of doing the right thing!

If this happens, the emptiness that you will feel can NEVER be filled with anything else! Unfortunately, many times in life, people fail to recognize the greatness of what they have, until it is lost!

To lose your lady is an exceptionally tough lesson to suffer through because it is our nature to believe that such a tragedy will not happen to us. However, there are plenty of examples that prove that we as men do push the outer limits of tolerance of our Special Lady.

When she is gone, the emptiness is unimaginable! The darkness and gloom that takes over one's life are inescapable. It becomes an unforgiving heavy burden of excruciating mental and emotional pain that seems to have no end in sight! I don't want that for anyone! That is why you now have this study-guide book in your possession so that you can correct the death spiral into the abyss of no return and SAVE your relationship with your Precious Lady!

My goal is to share with you the vital relationship salvaging actions and behaviors that you can implement right now! These suggestions and recommendations will help your lady see that you are transforming and becoming a new man.

So here is the deal; Let's work together and do our best to make sure that you do not lose your most precious and lovely lady.

How to Be a Better Dude Transformation Process

The first three chapters of this study-guide book are to get you familiar with some of the basic concepts of why our brain produces many of our thoughts, feelings, and emotions which cause us to treat our Precious Lady poorly at times.

There are some intriguing factual brain science insights contained within these chapters that show you how you can take advantage of the natural functioning processes of how your brain works as it relates to learning. These methods will assist you in the production of new thoughts, new behaviors, and an improved self-image.

Once you review this information, you will be able to clearly see how you can leverage how your brain works to create transformative growth within yourself. This leads to you treating the Love of Your Life with the best of heart, mind, and spirit every day.

The application of this information works because you are activating and expanding powerful new communication structures within your brain. This process of developing these new structures can alter "what" you think and "how" you act.

Whenever you repeatedly provide new information for your brain to learn, you create new "Dominant Mental Operating Programs" or Scripts within your brain that move your thoughts into a new direction. Eventually, these newly developed programs will govern more of what you think, how you act, and ultimately how well you "CHOOSE" to treat your most Precious Lady.

Gentlemen, get ready because this is going to be one intense, eye-opening, mind-expanding journey of self-discovery, personal growth, and development!

Insight X

How to Be a Better Dude and Treat Your Lady Right

Special Insight Letter from the Author to You!

If I could get inside of your brain, I would direct it right now to go to your most precious love and apologize for all the wrong that you have done to her.

I would like to be able to manipulate your brain so that you can feel the great pain and heartache that you have caused her. I would like to have you feel all the anguish and severe emotional trauma she had felt because of your rotten attitude, and your unacceptable and inexcusable behavior.

Well, we both know that I cannot do any of that, so, I must leave it up to you to do the right things. That is my hope! <u>Keep in mind when reading this material that I, at one time, was one mean, brutal hardcore kind of dude. One day, I realized that I was very wrong in virtually all of my thoughts, spoken words and actions, as it related to how to treat women and others. However, one day, I read something, I learned, and I changed. So, I stand before you today and say that you CAN grow and become a better man if that is your desire.</u>

For those of you that decided to make the change, your love life is about to soar to new, inexplicable and unimaginable heights of happiness and passion. **For those of you who don't change, you will get what you have sown from your careless thinking and reckless behavior.** I say good luck with those old defective thinking and behaviors patterns!

For all of you who decided to grow and become one who is counted as a "Real Man" by treating your lady right, I respect you for your efforts. Many other men around the world applaud you and admire your great efforts!

You are becoming part of an elite group of men who have chosen to live and speak in a better way by embracing the principles of "**How to Be a Better Dude and Treat Your Lady Right**" because they have realized that their "Special Lady" is ALWAYS worth it!

> *** **You do not need to be out there alone! When contacting me, you have reached out to a friend. Let's see if we can find a helpful solution together.**

Jeffrey K. Gadley

Jeff@HowToBeABetterDude.com

CHAPTER 1

Truth Exposed — Knowledge is Power

The Ugly Truth --- We Are All Programmed!

No matter who you are, your thoughts are a by-product of years of influences that started the day you were born. *The exception to the rule:* individuals with brain damage and with defects that cause chemical imbalances and deficiencies that cause mental issues. However, this is only a tiny percentage of the population.

Pay Close Attention: **How you treat your Special Lady is the direct by-product of WHAT you think and HOW you think.** What you think and how you think are a direct result of all the information programs that have been loaded into your brain from earliest beginnings of life. These programs or mental operating scripts were given to you by family, friends, teachers, clergy, movies, TVs and radio. Even as we have grown older, most of us STILL unconsciously give our brain over to these forces that have shaped us into who we are today.

I always wondered why I was so messed up in the head with the kind of thoughts that would come into my mind. But I had no clue until I accidentally looked into the rear-view mirror of my car while I was driving. I just had one of my nuclear-catastrophic insane road-rage meltdowns. That short two-second glance of my face and eyes, as I was foaming at the mouth and spewing hate, death and highly incendiary verbal insults at an elderly driver of the other vehicle showed me the pure ugliness of my heart. As much as I wanted to blame the innocent driver, I knew the real problem was me 100%! My attitude sucked BIG Time!

That glimpse of me in the mirror started me on a personal journey towards CHANGE! <u>What I saw in the mirror was pure EVIL!</u> It caused me to question WHY did I get so outraged when I became angry about ANYTHING?

"As I change my thoughts, the world around me begins to change."

Oh, It Gets Much Worse! One day, it dawned on me that I acted this way the majority of my life, whenever I was angry. Yes, even at my girlfriend at that time, I would blow-up in this similar fashion as described above. I was a total lunatic!

In this study-guide book, "How to Be a Better Dude and Treat Your Lady Right," my confession to you is that there is an extremely high probability that I have been at the point you are right now. In fact, I thoroughly used all the garbage language, anger, and disrespect towards family, friends, and loved-ones.

What I Discovered? My temperament was shaped by experiences, based on the way I was treated growing up with the combination of interactions of friends and showdowns with "mortal sworn-to-the-death enemies." In that mix was a lot of hard, rough language, violence, intimidation and people displaying anger and rage.

I unconsciously adopted these negative skill-sets, and displayed them, even during small little differences of opinion. So, once I started dating, I brought with me those same attitudes and behaviors. If I perceived that my girlfriend did something wrong, then I would unload with the full might and power of a blistering verbal beat-down that would leave her badly shaken.

How did I Change? Well, I changed the kind of information that I was allowing into my head. Anything negative — whether it came from family, friends, TV and the radio — I put them away from myself. I started reading information on how to self-improve, and how to get rid of all the burning anger, bitterness and rage.

From the first self-improvement book that I read, I could feel something happening inside of me that was good. I started having flashes of all the times in the past that I would get entirely out of control and then, suddenly, I realized that I could have controlled myself in each of those events.

Oh, it did not feel like it at that time it was happening, but without any hesitation or reservation, <u>I know that I am the one who is in control of my thoughts, my spoken words, and my behaviors</u>.

How Do You Make the Change? If you desire to change and become enlightened on How to Become a Better Dude, then I will boldly tell you right now: this study-guide book WILL help you to do so, as long as you repeatedly do the Mental Training Exercises contained within.

"I strive every day to improve myself and shower my lady with outward acts of love."

The double punch combination of your white-hot burning desire and repetition of the Mental Training Exercises are what will make your transformative growth occur.

On Your Journey… Watch Out for Your Nemesis.

Once you start to make changes in the way that you think, speak and behave, be fully aware that your greatest nemesis will challenge you to your success. That nemesis is the *old you*!

The *old you* want nothing to do with changing anything about you, and it will do everything in its power to thwart you and keep you just the same.

I am cautioning you right now to understand this because most of our long-term hardened mental programs do not like disruption of the old established patterns.

There are neurological and biochemical networks in your brain at work that seem to pull you into doing what you have always done (the old way). These old networks will tempt you to break your new routine of personal growth. This is not good!

That is why your level of desire must be extremely high, and you must practice the daily mental exercises and affirmation statements.

Your dedicated efforts of repetition and strong desire to improve are paramount to your success of becoming a better man for the Love of Your Life and learning all you need to learn on how to treat your lady right.

The #1 Enemy Against Your Personal Growth is YOU!

Truly, YOU are your own worst enemy! This is WHY you will find throughout this study-guide material; I will repeat these statements and concepts. I have also posted throughout the different kinds of Affirmation statements for you to embrace and live by, as you are learning.

You also will find that I keep on emphasizing the fact that you CAN make personal growth happen for you! No matter how long you have been stuck in a cycle of misery and poor decision-making as it relates to your Special Lady, you CAN turn it around — provided you keep on developing yourself.

"Treating my Lovely Lady with love and kindness every day is my mission."

The key is to perform the mental exercises consistently and to be exceptionally ambitious about being the New Best You that you can. Be motivated by it!

It takes work, but the task is always simple. You just have to keep on inputting new information into your brain, in the way of new Mental Operating Program Scripts and over a short amount of time, new thoughts will begin to surface.

With repetition, you CAN drown out the power of the *old you* and the nasty, unfavorable and abusive attributes of that identity.

It is called the **"Dilution Factor"** because you are diluting out the power of the old, well-established mental programs in your brain because you are steady at work building up new mental programs that serve you towards positive and inspiring thoughts and actions.

Chapter 2

Brain Science Insights

It is strongly advised that you study this chapter diligently. Once you have a clear understanding of the information in Chapter 2; it will be a gateway to a deeper understanding for gaining more insight with the remaining, what you can do to accelerate your personal growth, and why the application of the information works!

Who You are Today and Who Will You Become Tomorrow?

So, now you realize that you need to make some serious changes, to preserve the relationship with your Precious Lady or you want to improve who you are as a man because you recognized some things about yourself that were not favorable. I can relate because I was a little bit of both!

There are a lot of people out there who will tell you:

- that "*you cannot change*" or,
- they will say: "*that is just the way you are*" or,
- "*you can't change your personality.*"

Each One of the Above Statements is 100% FALSE!

If you can learn how to ride a bike, play a musical instrument or tie your shoes, then you can learn new habits that add positive attributes to you. You can learn how to get rid of negative thoughts and habits. **You CAN Custom-Design the *New You*!**

Research in the area of Neuro-Sciences has proven that the brain is similar in function to a computer, and the software could be viewed as your conscious and subconscious mind. Your subconscious mind controls vital aspects of your body functions, but it is also a massive recording and storage mechanism for ALL of Life's Experiences! Yeah, ALL of them! Whether you remember them or not, it has them.

The most important takeaway for you should be to understand who you are today and what you can become tomorrow, is due in part, to whatever dominant information is downloaded (put) into your conscious and subconscious mind. This is what has and will govern in the future, your thoughts, your speech, and your actions!

"The moment that I open my eyes from sleeping, I am thinking loving thoughts."

Simply put, if you have low-quality information repeatedly going into your conscious and subconscious mind, then you can expect low-quality responses to various circumstances in life. These will be expressed by your thoughts, your spoken words and then by your actions!

In the world of computers, the acronym is GIGO means Garbage In = Garbage Out! It all comes down to the programs that have been put in place by the programmer.

Beginning Now, YOU are the Master Programmer of Your Own Mind!

If you were to constantly stream high-quality Information into your conscious and subconscious mind, which is positive and uplifting; then guess what kind of thoughts your mind would eventually produce? **Answer:** Your mind would naturally generate positive and uplifting thoughts! Good stuff, man!

Generally speaking, positive thoughts are followed by positive actions in behavior. Here's the real deal: Whatever dominant programs (thoughts and activities) are taken in by your conscious and subconscious mind, eventually, this is what will start to rise to the level of your conscious thoughts.

In fact, 90% of all of your conscious thinking, speaking, being and doing arises from the subconscious mind. This means that we are all a by-product of all of life's experiences, and whatever dominant programs were reinforced in us. Over time, usually because of repetition, these thoughts are the ones that rise to the conscious mind and cause us to be as we are.

Brain Science Shows that you can acquire virtually any skill, adopt a new personality trait or break an old negative habit by infusing your mind with a steady, repeated flow of information that leads you to your goal. WOW!

I did not want to be a horrible man in life, so I made conscientious decisions to put high-quality information into my conscious and subconscious minds every day. I knew that I was one jacked-up dude and had a burning desire to change!

I knew I was not serving myself or my lady well. I was hair-trigger-irritable and impulsively angered by stupid stuff or getting mad at her and others for literally nothing! Bro, I am telling you that the problem, for the most part, was ME! I was moody, and I regularly had a bad attitude out of nowhere. So, I had to re-train my brain…FAST!

"I am kind, gentle and easy whenever I speak to my beautiful lady."

All my life, I was brainwashed into believing that the way I acted was something that I was stuck with or that it was okay because nobody is perfect.

How blind I was to the truth. What a bunch of crap!

Once I fully realized that I had to correct some personality defects <u>and that it was possible</u>, I aggressively went to work and dumped into my brain tremendous amounts of Information along the lines of self-image improvement. I began to form better communication while learning how to express love in the very best of ways — not only by my words but by my actions.

This study-guide book is all about becoming a better man. It's how to treat your lady like the Princess or Queen of your world. However, because the information is so enlightening, you will discover that it can be applied to ANY area of your life, as long as your desire is robust, as you strive to have personal growth and outstanding success.

Since I believe this book is so critical to understanding how you can redesign yourself and kill off destructive and corrupted mental operating programs, I am going to break down its many concepts into detail. This is to show you how the transformation process works in helping you to become the person who you sincerely want to be.

This growth will not only impact you, but it will cause your Special Lady to see that you are a changed man at the very core of your being.

"Class is in Session!" Grab a pen and paper or write in your study-guide book, but take some notes. Learn this process! If you learn it and then apply it, it WILL create for you spectacular life-changing possibilities.

Ready - Set - Let's Go!

Within your brain, there are highly specialized learning and communication cells called "Neurons." **<u>They are the means, by which all of us learn EVERYTHING!</u>**

They are responsible for trillions of calculations and communications in your body EVERY SECOND! Your brain has over 100 BILLION of these specialized communication cells.

"I lead every day of my life by showing my precious lady love and affection."

Brain neurons are highly versatile when it comes to learning and assimilating information, which helps you to become very good at anything that you are subjected to repeatedly.

Think about when you first attempted to ride a bike; your brain's neurons went to work to assist you in that skill. The more you tried to ride, the more proficient you became. This is because your neurons were steady at work locking-in your new talent and communicating with other neurons to help out with the task. The more you rode the bike, the higher your ability became. Those few neurons formed an entire communication network called a Neural-Network. **The individual neurons actually wire together due to your repeated efforts to develop the ability to ride the bike proficiently.** *(Look mom, no hands!)*

This is what your brain does whenever you are learning ANYTHING! Cool, huh?

The bad news is that the process is exactly the same, whether you are learning something good or learning something highly-negative. *Example:* Individuals who become proficient at being a criminal have developed a Neural-Network for specific skills that help them with their trade of criminality.

The Rule is virtually anything that we regularly repeat and have a desire to succeed in, we can develop a Neural-Network that helps us to do it exceptionally well.

For a moment, think about the world of sports and music. Those individuals have developed those powerful communication networks (Neural-Networks) that allow them to be among the best in their field.

The very intriguing aspect of this is that we can learn things that negatively or positively affect us on a psychological or mental level and not even be consciously aware of it.

Take, for example, the words of a song. You do not have to be focused on it, but your brain can learn it just by hearing it repeatedly and then out of nowhere, you are either humming or singing the words effortlessly. Music also has the ability to move your soul emotionally and cause you to "feel" a certain way. In fact, this is an excellent example of unconsciously learning or programming your brain.

Information flows into our brain through our five senses, whether we are aware of it or not. And, for the most part, we are not aware of most of the information going into our brain. Consciously, we can only process a fraction of what is going in!

"I will always treat my precious lady well in all circumstances of life."

What You Think, Say and Do. Here is how it all relates to us developing the kind of thoughts we have, including what we say and what we do. They are ALL LEARNED! That means that we have established dominant communication networks for our thinking and behavior. Through repeated exposure to life's experiences, we have developed various attitudes, thinking and behavior patterns. These attitudes, thoughts and behavior patterns, in most cases, are nothing more than habits.

As far as your neurons are concerned, they do not care if the habit or behavior that you have developed to handle situations is a negative source or a positive one! Your brain just goes to work, to wire in your responses from the repeated exposure to the stimulus. If you are exposed to a stimulus repeatedly, or it is highly traumatic, then it could become a Dominant Mental Operating Program. You will get darn good at handling it with automatic responses from your Neural-Network!

Think about the skills of an elite boxer, such as a mix-martial expert or a Kung-Fu master. They have developed masterful skills through the development of neurons that continually relayed information to each other and formed a Neural-Network with highly energetic, automatic, reflex responses whenever they sense any act of aggression towards them. Their Neural-Networks have been so well trained that it just fires-off automatically to protect and defend!

This part really sucked for me. From life's early experiences, I developed skills for being mean, aggressive, lashing out, threatening, road rage with intent to beat the hell of out someone. I had a fear of authority, prejudice, irritability, flash-anger, intimidation, and swearing. Get it guys?

I had developed powerful Neural-Networks for all of this garbage, so that they were put on display whenever I felt threatened on ANY level, physically or mentally. It did not matter who it was that I was reacting to!

All of my ways to communicate and defend my fragile self-image were all channeled through Negative-Neural-Networks. These systems were set up within me from early in life. Sadly, I can remember some of the experiences that brought about my most negative thoughts, speech, actions, and behaviors.

A Revolution Inside of Me. It was an incredible feeling to me once I learned why I acted-out so many times with intense aggression and had negative thoughts streaming through my head virtually all the time. Freedom was now in sight!

"The NEW me has arrived in full force, and love leads all of my actions."

Once I discovered that I could re-wire my brain and re-design myself, it was a game-on! I was pumped up and said to myself, "Get out of my freakin' way, because a New Man is coming to town!"

I started a revolution within myself and went on a mission to accelerate my personal growth to levels that I would not have thought were possible.

<u>**I am hoping that it does the same for you as you apply the information!**</u>

This study-guide book CAN assist you in stimulating neurons in your brain through repeated actions and exposure to this information. Consistent training of your mind causes your neurons to strengthen their connections to assist in the formation of new Positive Neural-Networks within your brain. Your woman will love it!

Science shows that: "neurons that begin to fire together eventually will wire together." It is this wiring together of these neurons that cause **new thoughts** to rise to the surface of your conscious mind. <u>The old, corrupted, negative Neural-Networks begin to lose their power over you.</u>

WHY? Because neurons that no longer fire together, no longer have a need to wire together. <u>This decreases the influence of the neural-network, and you start to cause weakness in the power of the habit.</u>

Good habits and bad habits are broken in the same way. Once you start decreasing the signals to the Neural-Network through lack of use, over time, the network tends to lose its wiring together. Remember the expression: Use it or Lose it? ;-)

A good example is this: if you have ever played a musical instrument with a moderate degree of proficiency and then stopped practicing for a week or two, you know that you have lost that razor-sharp edge. The less you do it, then the more weakened and less responsive the Neural-Network becomes.

It is this same process of how you learn EVERYTHING, whether it is a good thing or a bad thing the process is basically the same.

As you are learning, just keep in mind that you have a very Special and Precious Lady out there waiting for the man of her dreams to walk through the door today.

At one time, that man was you, but by now things have changed. You now have in your hand's information that can help you make the most amazing transformative growth and development. The power of that decision to reshape who you are and again, become that man of her dreams and more, is yours and yours alone!

"I choose to put healthy, good quality information into my brain every day."

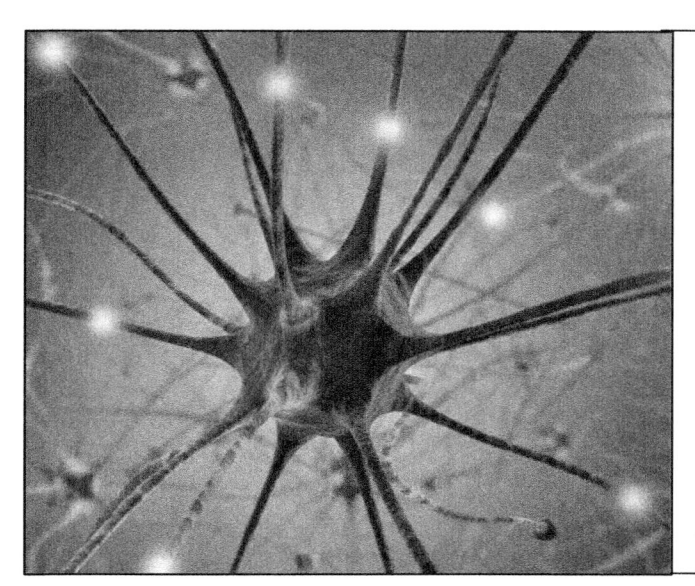

Graphic illustration of a single neuron in the brain. When stimulated by learning new information, it releases bio-chemicals and can incorporate other neurons to assist in the learning process.

When you seek personal growth and development the more you learn, more of these neurons eventually join forces to assist you in your mission.

See down below.

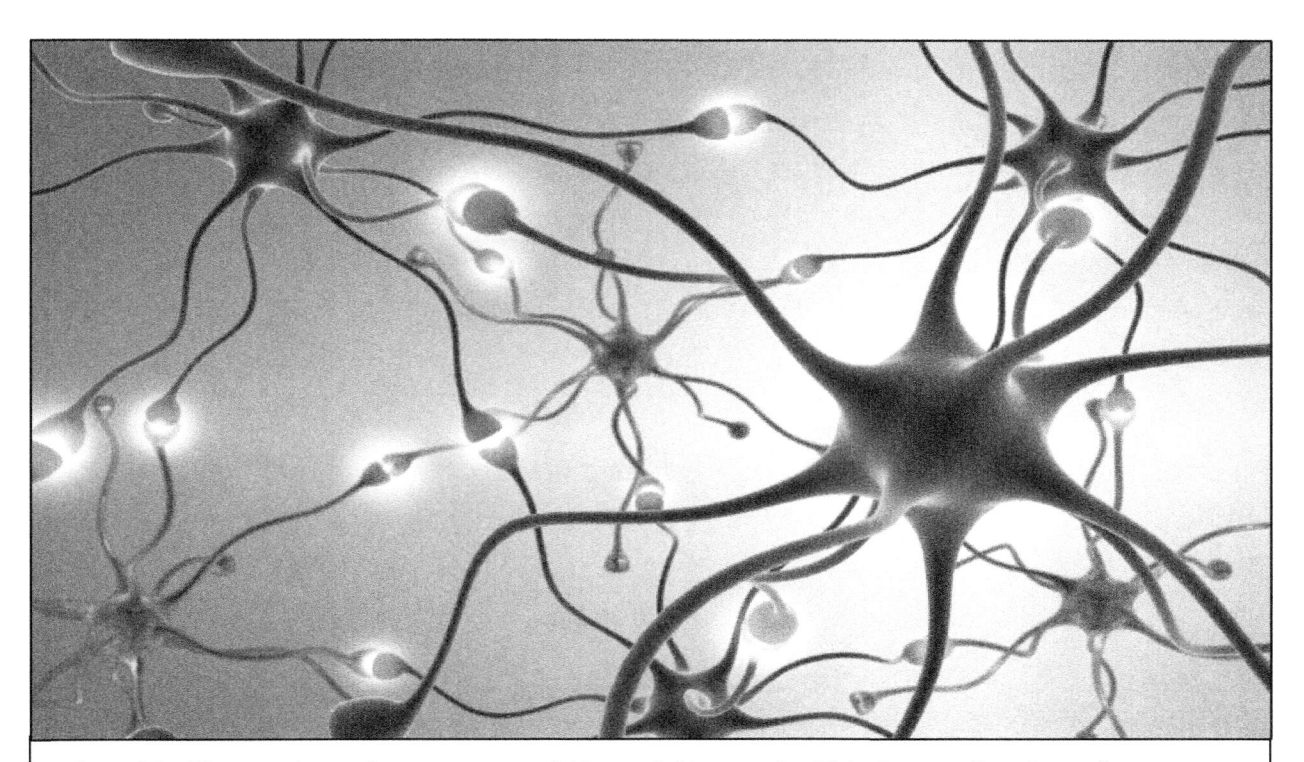

Graphic illustration of a connected Neural-Network. This is a collective of neurons that have communicated and wired together for the purpose of assisting in learning of new information. The more one practices and continues to learn a specific thing, this network becomes a powerful unit of perfection. Whether your learning is positive or negative, good or bad, it all works the same. *Choose Positive and Good.*

"As a New Man, I always speak kindly to my lovely lady."

CHAPTER 3

Choose How You Want to Be

Who in the world likes being miserable in a relationship? Not me! The chances are that you don't want to be in a broken-down relationship, which is full of negative energy and drama. However, the problem is rampant throughout the world. Men and women argue and fight in mass numbers because of lack of communication or communication that is unacceptably poor!

The other thing that I have learned is that when men are frustrated and become angry in their relationship, they come at their woman with massive amounts of heated and assaulting language.

If you are reading this, then you most likely know what I am talking about. It seems as though our mouth goes into hyper-drive and we can go absolutely berserk in expressing our displeasure with her. As the relationship goes on, without intervention or relationship classes, these high-voltage verbal abuses only become magnified. We have spoken harshly to our lady that we damage (or sometimes wholly destroy) her self-worth. The result of this kind of repeated abuse by us. She can feel demoralized and rotten to her core.

My friend, You and I are the ones to blame for being so mean and hurtful to our Precious and Lovely Lady. We eagerly stand up on our soap-box, and with our intimidating physical posture and harsh words, we start blasting away at her! We let loose with a verbal, and sometimes physical attack in order to dominate the scene with an ugly flow of crude and hate-filled language.

The Truth Is that it does not have to be this way! There is a way out of this cycle of destruction IF you elect to choose a different path for your relationship.

The time is NOW. You should make the change before you lose the Love of Your Life for good!

We all have the power of choice in this manner! My recommendations are quite simple as you go forward through the pages of this book. Choose the path that leads to love and harmony in your relationship.

"Today, right now, I am a better man – I treat my lady with loving kindness every day."

This means making the conscious decision using the power of choice to cease all arguments! This means using the power of choice to say kind words to your lady! This means learning to use the power of choice to lift-up and build-up each other every single day.

We, as men, are capable of so many beautiful, positive and inspiring actions. Sadly, we are also capable of the most violent and destructive acts imaginable to the human race, especially to the Love of Our Life.

I am challenging you right now here today. Use your power of choice to allow only words of love and kindness to flow from your lips when speaking to your Special Lady.

If you claim that you love her, then you know that what I am asking is a simple task. For what does the word "Love" mean? Does it equate to speaking harshly or rudely to your beautiful and loving lady? I think not! Does it mean putting her down or swearing and yelling at her? Nope, that is wrong, any day and at any time! **These kinds of actions are ALWAYS unacceptable behavior!**

Are You a Real Man? A real man is secure in himself. He does not have to resort to such destructive verbal assaults and character assassinations to the woman whom he loves.

Your gut feelings and you know that I am right! So, it is time to "Man-up" and end that crap right now — at this very second!

It is vital to keep in mind that the overall mission of this book is to teach all men who read it to lead with love, even when you don't feel like it or even if it is not your fault.

> *** Warning! ***
> Kiss your relationship good-bye, if your choice is to keep on going down the path of destructive words, actions and behaviors with that Super-Star Special Lady in Your life!

If you want to learn how to be a real man, then you need to change the way you are currently thinking. I vigorously suggest that you adopt a new attitude and manner of being. It can all start right now, this very day! *** **You need to learn to cherish and adore that Special Lady at all times!**

"I only speak gently, easy and relaxed."

BRAIN TRAINING

Your First Brain Training Assignment is on the Next Page.

This simple routine will begin the process of building a new neural-network for you, that gradually improves your thoughts and actions. **Desire, Emotion and Repetition are Paramount to Your Success.**

- Read it to yourself 10-12 times per day for the next two days.
- On the third day, speak it outwardly multiple times throughout the day.
- Always Perform with Focus - No Distractions!
- Turn OFF the radio and put that damn cell phone down!
- Read two times as you awaken. BEFORE you get out of bed.
- Read two times during your morning coffee and/or morning work breaks.
- Make a quick phone call during the day and tell your lady something loving.
- Send her one or two texts that express words of endearment to her daily.
- Read the New Man Trainer twice BEFORE walking in the door to greet your lady.
- Greet your lady with a warm, tender embrace when coming through the door.
- NEVER walk through the door on your cell phone. Full attention directed at her.
- Read two times before you go to bed and contemplate the words spoken.
- Always read with intense feelings of emotion. Make yourself feel it deep!

Be energetic in your efforts to learn, grow, and implementation at all times!

Words of Caution: If you are lazy with your Mental Brain Exercises or your desire is lukewarm, YOU WILL FAIL to acquire the personal growth and development that is necessary for you to promote healing within yourself and your broken relationship.

I have found that the best way to approach this new experience of re-wiring your brain is to do so with an extreme enthusiast attitude. **Learning is enhanced when your emotions are heavily invested** in your actions. Make sure you have the "I CAN" mindset, and you WILL succeed.

It is also imperative to know that the more often you do these kinds of Mind Trainer Exercises, then the faster the new thoughts and creativity begin to become a part of the *New You*.

"I am a New Man as I begin my journey to become better as a man."

Today is a New Day for Me to Show

New Man Mind Trainer # 1

Today is a New Day for me to show _____, the very best of who I am. I am a New Man, and today represents a New Beginning. In this New Beginning, before I leave the house, I'll go to _____, and hold her and tell her that she means the world to me.

Today, I create new thoughts within my head that are of Praise, Gentleness and a Relaxed-Easy Flowing mind. I'll ALWAYS be kind and gentle to my Precious Lovely Lady. Today, I praise her, and I thank God in Heaven for her!

Today is a New Beginning, and I am a New Man. As a New Man, I think of her FIRST and search out ways to bring a smile to her face. I am mindful and helpful. I figure out simple acts of kindness, that I can do to warm her soul.

When I come home to see _____, I'll greet her with an abundance of appreciation upon seeing her face. I'll greet her with love, patience and a heart that adores and cherishes her. I am a New Man. I am a New Man who is getting better every day. I choose to be of good-heart and a gentle spirit EVERY DAY! I am a New Man! *(end of affirmation)*

Tip: Focus and put strong emotion into your thinking and your spoken words whenever you practice your scripts. Once you are speaking the New Man Mind Trainer scripts out loud; be bold about it, be excited. Embrace every word and statement that you speak with emotion and now see yourself living by your words.

Yes, even when I get in front of the mirror and practice speaking the words out loud to YOURSELF!

The sound of your own voice being heard when repeated consistently helps to re-wire your brain and moves you closer to the goal of your transformation mission statement.

"I am a New Man as I begin my journey to become better as a man."

Tough Talk Ahead Through the Next 8 Chapters

Guys, this will be down-to-earth and realistic talk. It exposes the problem that I believe is rampant throughout the world. I am cautioning you UPFRONT to know that I am hard on us because I have seen varying levels of abuse on women by us (men) my whole life! Try not to be personally offended by my words and tone at times. I will admit that sometimes they are blunt and cut right to the heart of the problem. I speak intensely against the kind of behavior, where a man will verbally trash-out his Precious Love with blistering anger-rich, demeaning and degrading statements that serve the sole purpose to brutalize emotionally. This kind of behavior by most standards is considered EVIL! It isn't right on any level, bro!

Just remember, the next several chapters are tough. Along the way, I do offer immediate corrective action-oriented steps so that you can implement *At the Speed of Your Thoughts* to begin the process of healing the wounds of the relationship.

Also, keep in mind that I am one of those men who used to be blind to the destruction I was creating, as well as the emotional pain that I handed out. I was clueless about how I was and thought that hardcore manhood was established by being a jerk to my woman.

Though, I hope none of you are as bad as I was. I do speak with a lot of force on this matter because I was thoroughly awakened one day on how wrong I was for being the kind of person I was. But, I did correct the errors, and this material will help you do the same.

With all that as being said, let's get busy with your study-guide book on "**How to Be a Better Dude and Treat Your Woman Right.**"

"I only adopt positive, healthy new attitudes, thoughts and actions."

CHAPTER 4

How Did We Get So Jacked-up in the First Place?

Have you ever wondered how we got so grossly screwed-up in our thoughts and actions towards women? I have, so get ready for the truth. This is something that they are not going to teach you in school.

It all starts with our self-image. Our self-image begins to develop from infancy, with the input from the world around us. It doesn't matter if the information was positive or negative. Your subconscious mind was hard at work permanently recording and storing all the information that you were being exposed to.

With the input of all this information, we started on a path to create a concept or an image of who we are and what we are capable of being. These thoughts of self will be influenced initially by those who raised us and have strong influences on our lives.

In our early years of our development, we have no prior knowledge or experience to use as a guide for building a healthy self-image. The only material that you had available to you to create your self-image was what you experienced and took in from your five senses, but primarily, from what you saw and heard. **Whether the information was good or bad, true or false, real or fake ---- you used this information as the basis for determining what you would believe about yourself.**

A multitude of times, the information that you received about yourself was NOT true! If you ever heard anyone say something negative about you, even though it is not true, you may have come to believe that it is true. You would use this as the basis for building up specific ideas about yourself.

Highly Sensitive Role Models (HSRM) such as our parents and closest friends, ALL can play a part in the concepts that we develop about ourselves.

Usually, the individuals that we look up to with an enormous amount of respect, admiration, and love; their words and opinions can carry massive influence over what we think of ourselves. Highly Sensitive Role Models can shatter us into a million pieces with just one disapproving look or grunt.

"My mind is searching for things that I can do to make her smile today."

If we heard them say something about us that was not favorable, then we often times and automatically come to accept it as fact. In our mind, we will usually draw a hyper-sensitive, unfavorable conclusion about what we heard and then believe it, even when it is not true!!!

By the time we get old enough to break away from those early life influences of Highly Sensitive Role Models, we have become quite comfortable in our belief systems regarding who we are. So, here we go; off into life with damaged and scarred self-images that many times bring forth negative self-imposed, self-limiting, self-defeating thoughts and behaviors.

If you are the kind of man that is abusive to your lovely lady, or you are mean, grumpy, moody and angry — the chances are very high that it is because your experiences in life had those kinds of subconscious dominant mental operating programs governing your thoughts and behavior from long ago!

If your early years were anything similar to mine (I hope not), then the quality of information going into your brain was far from being high-quality-positive information for the most part.

Since you only know what you know, this is what your brain works with!

If you are given instructions, feedback, criticism, discipline, encouragement, and expressions of love and gentleness --- depending on the mix of those qualities, there is a strong possibility, they became the basis for how you think, speak and behave today. Let me not sugar-coat it for you. Your intent to be thoughtless, inconsiderate, rude and speak to your spouse or significant other rudely, abrasively, unkindly and harshly AT ANY TIME is because that is what you learned.

Those are the **Dominant Mental Operating Programs** of your brain. You act selfishly because you learned to be selfish. You act unkindly because you learned to be unkind. You act mean at times because that was what you learned. You act bitter, have temper-tantrums, cheat, curse, yell, scream, degrade, demean, lie, bully, manipulate and intimidate because all of these are what you learned as your best line of thought when handling the challenges of life!

Oh my, how I hated hearing all of that upon first hearing it! I think the reason I hated hearing that I had learned to be that way, so much is that those words spoke a great truth to my inner soul.

"I am re-programming my mind every day for expressing only positive actions."

<u>Those words cut me open to expose the true condition of my heart.</u> Then, I saw similar words in the Bible one day, and it shook me to my core!

<u>Important Note</u>: Whenever I say these negative attitudes are learned, keep in mind that the majority of our learning and absorption of information takes place unconsciously. This means we were not fully aware of the kind of information going into our subconscious mind most of the time, and the influence it is having on us.

In our early-life stages, it makes sense that we may not be aware of the kind of information going into our mind and how it influences our behavior. As we become young adults, we seem to reinforce early-life learned responses, both the good and bad ones. Then, finally, through the reckless process of Careless Inattention, we bring on additional influences of behavior. Yep! You just are not paying attention to the kind of information going into your brain! So, you now allow almost anything and everything in!

Do you remember that old computer software program acronym G.I.G.O.? It stands for Garbage in = Garbage Out.

You act irresponsibly because you learned how to be that way. **You Are What You Think, and it usually shows itself outwardly by what comes out of your mouth. Then, it is followed by your actions, behaviors, and habits.**

> *The good man brings good things out of the good treasure of his heart, and the evil man brings evil things out of the evil treasure of his heart. For out of the overflow of the heart, the mouth speaks.* Luke 6:45
>
> This Bible verse caused me to look at myself hard

Sadly, for many of us, our parents were not the best role models. However, in their defense, it is because they too, were the victims of garbage information being dumped into their mind by those who raised them, and their experiences early in life!

The real ugly truth is this: this way of learning can be a hellacious repeating cycle of negative programming that is passed down generation to generation.

However, this by no means gets you off the hook for treating the Lady of Your Life with so little regard for her feelings. Now is the time to gain life-changing insight into why you treat her so poorly.

In case you have not figured it out; you treat your Precious Lady with disrespect and a cruel heart because <u>you have LEARNED to be that way!</u>

"I am always seeking the kindest words and actions that lift my woman's heart."

Unfortunately, in our early years of life, for most, we do not get the correct high-quality information on how to treat a woman and how to praise her up.

Until we are awakened to the truth, we unknowingly go about <u>Unconsciously Unaware</u> of what we are thinking and how we are acting.

Thus, if there is no awakening our self, then we are doomed to a life of negative and corrupted speech and behavior. These are the Dominant Mental Operating Programs of our brain. These programs, in essence, have made us who we are today.

Consider this your wake-up call!

Hello!

I am blaring the warning sirens! I am slapping you upside hard-head with a caring heart, bro to bro! Fix this problem (You). NOW!

<u>**Guys, this is ALL learned behavior!**</u>

It is not cast in stone, and it <u>CAN</u> be corrected! You do not have to accept these kinds of negative and destructive thoughts, actions and behaviors.

You Do Have a Way Out!

Even as you read this paragraph, combined with your deep burning desire and willingness to change, it sets into motion the new learning neurons of your brain that can set you on the path to becoming a New Man!

I will present much more information on this as you continue to read, but for now, let me provide you with a few questions on the next page to gain a bit more clarity into how we get to be screwed up as dudes in the first place.

"I am filling my heart with words and acts that show my great love for my lady."

☐ Did anyone ever provide you with long-term education and coaching in the area of how you should treat a woman? (*Not for me did it happen!*)

☐ Did anyone ever provide you education or ongoing training on how you should communicate with a woman and listen to what her heart is "REALLY" saying? (*I had no clue I was supposed to listen to anything she said.*)

☐ Did you ever receive any training or education in school or at home, in the art of communication, that you should NEVER yell, scream, curse, demean and speak harshly or recklessly to the woman they you "SAY" that you love so much and care about? (*I always yelled and cursed at everybody.*)

☐ Did anyone ever sit you down to teach you about personally developing yourself and self-improving on how you think, and what you think? (*Nope, and I thought that my thinking was perfectly fine anyway. Thank you very much!*)

☐ Has anyone ever told you that you could rewire your brain and change to become the man of her dreams again, and showed you how to begin the process of this Life-Changing Transformative Process? (*What the hell is that?*)

If you are a man who wants to change and improve yourself on how you treat the most precious and special person of your life, then this information is perfect for you to begin the process.

A bit more about how we acquire our "Good Man Training."

As men, NORMALLY we get our information on how we treat our lady by seeing how our fathers treated our mom. During our teenage years, we saw and received additional information and influences from outside sources. (LOOK OUT!) And, this is where things usually get really twisted in our minds. We met older boys and young men who told us what they did to girls, and how we are to treat them.

Then, we saw in movies and heard the songs on the radio, which further educate us on how to be a super cool dude. Finally, all hell broke loose because we got exposed to pornography and beer/alcohol! Oh no! From that point, our brains have been downloaded with information so intense that the impressions can misguide us for the rest of our lives.

You may ask the question or wonder, is it all really so bad?

The answer is "YES" and here is why. Ninety percent of ALL conscious thoughts arise from the subconscious mind. The subconscious mind is <u>always absorbing information</u> from all our five senses, and it has no built-in filter to determine whether the information coming in is good or bad. So, if you have received dark, negative information repeatedly regarding anything in life, then the thoughts that eventually arise and start to dominate your thinking are those kinds of thoughts.

Your thoughts affect your speech in terms of WHAT you say, and HOW you say what you say when you speak to everyone. Your thoughts determine the language you will use, and how harsh you will be in your delivery of those words. Your thoughts determine the actions and behaviors that you will bring forth in any given set of circumstances.

Since you are a by-product of what you know and what you don't know, you are most likely to bring forth the accumulation of years of ugliness that you have absorbed from your environment, and from **Highly Sensitive Roles Models** in your life.

In a close personal relationship with your Precious Lady who you love, you also are most likely to display that negative and ugly side of your thoughts and behavior to her, while she did not have anything to do to your irritation or frustration!

Those who were Highly Sensitive Role Models (HSRM) in my life, for the most part, taught me the worst of the worst. When it came to girls, and my environment in my teens, I learned how to be one mean, tough dude to everyone — including women.

My thoughts regarding women and how to treat them were born primarily right out of hell! Growing up in the hood, and hanging out with my tainted, screwed-up "in the hood" older role models gave me a thought platform of hard, harsh, bitter, vindictive, demean, curse-out, degrade and go to hell mentality!

> **YES... even with all of my negative ways of thinking, speaking and being, I thought, I was an okay kind of guy.**

"I greet my day with gratitude. I truly do appreciate my Precious Love."

Exposure to Massive Doses of Pornography XXX

Many boys/men receive intense mental stimulation of what a woman is supposed to be all about by absorbing massive doses of pornography daily. For many, this comes in the form of pornographic pictures, movies, and apps with easy phone access and in voluminous amounts! With easy access to it and the repeated act of seeing it over and over, it can imprint long-lasting, intense images in their minds. And now, they go off into the world looking to fulfill on a lot of what they have seen.

In essence, like the song says: "**Baby, I just want to bust your stuff**." In a young man's mind that is highly impressionable and easily manipulated, this is a part of the self-indoctrination process of learning what a woman is all about. The bottom-line is this: This is part of what we as men learned in terms of why women should be pursued. This is how they should be "handled" according to music and role models.

Even if you had great role models and excellent teachings on such matters, once you catch the pornographic images on your screen, you ARE TOAST! Your mind gets WARPED! The imagery is incredibly powerful, and those images have a very high stick-ability factor within your thoughts! Recurring thoughts! Night-time dream thoughts! Day-time dream thoughts! Anytime dream thoughts!

Has anyone ever come to those young and highly impressionable minds and said, "A woman should be treated like a Princess, and talked to with only words of kindness and gentleness?" NO WAY! Why? Because almost every one of those roles models is the same exact way as the youngsters are. **Screwed Up and severely lacking in quality information and wisdom regarding women!**

Exposure to Women Being Degraded in Music, Movies, and Art

Now we stir the pot a little bit more by listening to music that demeans and degrades women. Young boys start hearing and singing from memory from about the age three years old because they hear it repeatedly! Unconscious learning is at work here.

Seriously, what in the hell do you think is going to happen to a mind that was brainwashed with filth, and taught with repeated themes of kicking a woman's a**, if she does not listen and "telling that b_tch to shut up the f_ck up?"

"I CHOOSE only good thoughts because they heal the heart of my precious lady."

I have listened carefully over the years to the lyrics of songs especially rap, rock, and metal; unfortunately, many are not kind towards women, and directly instruct men on how to feel about them or how to "handle" them!

THINK! Put this together with just regular standard Television shows and the big screen cinema movies. You can EASILY see that there is a steady flow of violence, rape, degradation, and other brutalities acted on towards women.

This kind of consistent input of GARBAGE into the brain is shaping the attitudes of men and their thoughts and behaviors towards women!

Yet, our society runs out and says: "Aw man, that was a great movie!" Or they say: "How cool a song that was," though it was trashing women, and not really paying attention to the impact that it was making to their minds or a child's mind.

I mean, what the heck was going on? Sadly, in today's world, they give significant awards of recognition for the kind of filth and mind-warping crap that I just outlined above. You know what I am saying is 100% TRUE!

Though some would argue that it is "just a movie" or it is "just a song" or that "It is not real," here is what you need to know... your subconscious mind does not know if it is real or not. It cannot determine that it is "just a song!"

The subconscious mind's job is to record that information given to it by our five senses and reference it for later use. Repeated exposure increases the signal strength for the use of this garbage information at some future point and time. Yeah, that is the real deal; get it into your head right now. This is no joke, and you need to take it all with intense seriousness.

When our conscious and subconscious minds acquire this kind of information with years of influence, what do you really believe that a young man will surely be like at the core of his heart? <u>From what I have seen and personally experienced, many times our brains have been warped negatively</u>. If push comes to shove, it's easy to generate "not so nice" thoughts towards women. In fact, in an instant, we categorize them as b_tches, whores, and sluts. And, we are taught that she cannot be trusted!

Can anyone tell me, anywhere along the way, where young boys learn how to build up and praise young ladies? Generally speaking, it does not happen!!

"The words that I speak are full of life and love for my Lovely Lady."

Men are primarily the by-product of years of ruthless assaults on their young highly absorbable and easy to shape minds by media at every level. Specifically, by those who push garbage or junk media! Which includes TV, radio, news, advertisers, movies and music. Now, just imagine the combination of the pornographic pictures, movies with sound, rap, and metal music. Then, the constant bombardment of consistent and persistent direct peer influence, all coming together in this process. You can start to understand why men get so screwed up and do not know how they should think of a woman or how to communicate with her heart effectively.

A man's most basic and natural communication seems to come through his desire to have sex with any and all women he has interest in. Like it or not, that seems to be the result of years of research, and everyday life itself seems to bear that out.

By the time he finds the one for whom that he really cares, he is TOTALLY clueless in the art of communication to a woman's heart! He never developed the proper skills for healthy, and vibrant communication in the first place!

Many times, when a man attempts to break out of the traditional mode of poor treatment of a Special Lady, and some of our friends and associates find out about it, they start teasing and hammering on us. They tell us that we are weak, pussy-whipped, a weenie, gay or stupid!!!

I distinctly remember the multitude of times other men, would see me writing love notes to my girlfriend in my earlier years. I got a severe tongue-lashing because in their thoughts, for real men don't write love letters and cute little notes. It was labeled as too corny and wimpy. In their view, real men don't do such things.

Instead, real men go to the bars for picking-up girls!

Or, they go out drinking with a group of other men and get drunk, or off to the topless bar or a gentlemen's club to gawk and drool over dancing women. The whole stupid thing about this is that they foolishly throw their money away for some partially nude dancing babe in front of them.

"I CHOOSE actions that uplift and praise the strengths of my beautiful lady."

Wait a freakin' minute! Have we lost our minds? I would gladly throw my $20-dollar bill to My Princess, instead of some woman who I do not know or care about!

Before You Can Fix This Problem, You Must Understand It!

In most situations, the truth is that you MUST have an excellent understanding of the problem if you intend to fix it. So, allow me to be blunt. Generally speaking, we as men, are selfish, thoughtless and inconsiderate.

Many times, when a serious discussion arises between a man and woman in a relationship, men typically get angry and verbally FIGHT using insulting words. Unfortunately, it is usually all downhill from there. Next, we go in with a full-frontal assault to seek out and do intense emotional harm.

Of course, this does not apply to all men, but a whole lot of them out there are brutal and hard on their Special Lady. Bottom-line: She ends up being treated worse than sewer waste by-products!

The woman, whom you love, is waiting for you to wake up! She is being ripped to pieces emotionally. She does not understand why you are so mean, angry, grumpy, and demanding of her. She is horrified once you go on a yelling tirade cursing at her, belittling her, berating her, calling her all kinds of evil names, and hurling exceptionally painful insults!

BIG Freakin' Clue! This is no way to treat your Special Lady.

We know very little of self-sacrifice. We have this deep-rooted belief that we cannot say these three little words; ***"I am sorry."***

The Truth of the matter is that the Lady of Your Life should be treated as if there are no other women on the planet earth! You should be like a laser-beam of light focused on her and her needs, wants and desires.

You can easily ignore want I am saying. Most of you will, but the truth is quite simple**. Most of us ARE SCREWED UP**, and we need to change our ways. First, we have to load new high-quality information into our brains that improve our thoughts.

New information has the power to naturally rewire your brain, starting a positive and powerful transformative self-liberating change within you.

That new information that I am speaking of is all contained in the reading and regular application of the information in this study-guide book.

"I am the master of my thoughts - I no longer give in to my evil thoughts like a slave."

The regular use of Mental Mind Exercises contained within this book can move you more in the direction of where you want to go, by providing your mind with high-quality new information to process on a consistent basis.

Your desire and effort, even at this moment, is already beginning the process of rewiring your brain and improving your thoughts. You are essentially creating a biochemical reaction within your brain neurons that will continue to grow for your intended purpose of becoming a better man.

If you are ready to self-improve and save your relationship with your precious and beautiful lady, then continue with your high-impact, life-changing studies on How to Become a Better Dude!

> **On the next page** is a Special Report Segment that I have decided to enter into this study guide book at the last minute. Since I used to be an avid music listener, as well as a DJ at a tiny college I attended in upstate New York, I felt this study-guide book would not be complete in laying out all the steps that I took to de-program myself, from a corrupted, negative, and toxic mindset.
>
> I made the determination that this section of information could be highly critical, in optimizing your chances of success in your journey towards self-improvement and enriching your personal development.
>
> To further your understanding of this information that I am sharing with you, some insight into the unconscious and inattentive subconscious programming of our brain and how music, radio, and television play a role in shaping your thoughts.
>
> Though nearly everyone on the planet is heavily tied to music/radio and television, I am pointing out that if you are intense about making a change in your thoughts and behaviors, you may want to consider the role that such electronic devices of entertainment have, in providing messages into your brain that do not favor your ambitions to self-improve.

"I put good information into my brain, and this produces good thoughts."

CHAPTER 5

SPECIAL REPORT

Quick Word Regarding TV, Radio, and Music...

I cannot remember a time in my adult life where I paid attention to hearing my own inner voice speak to me. This was because I was ALWAYS listening heavily to some kind of electronic entertainment device. It would be entirely accurate to say that nearly all the programming of my mind was done by other people and electronic entertainment devices. The two primary ones were the radio and TV. **I do not believe that I ever thought clearly until I shut-down about 50% of my TV and movie viewing, and 95% of my radio listening.**

I grew up with those BIG three devices until cell phones and computers came into the mix. My mind was wholly absorbed into them nearly 24 hours a day! I would always go to sleep with the radio on and then listen to it in the car EVERY time that I drove somewhere. I would turn on the TV the moment I walked through the door, just to have it playing as background noise. **Then, at other times, I would have both the TV and radio on at the same time!** *What is up with that anyway?*

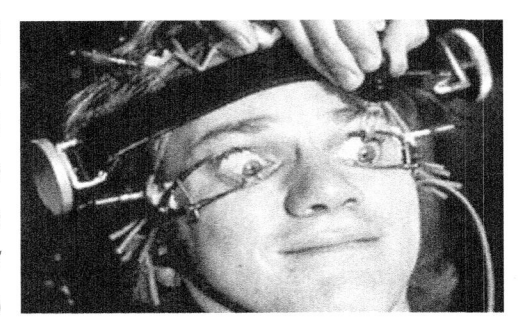

My point is that I ALWAYS had something drowning out my more profound thoughts. I had unknowingly kept myself unconsciously unaware of how I was as a person. I was always tuned-in or plugged-in to a constant source of music, TV, and movies because that is what I learned was the way to find peace and enjoyment.

Though entertainment devices and TV shows are supposed to be for comfort and relaxation, I discovered three critical life-changing revelations when I dramatically reduced my use of them.

The first thing: I could sense that I was being programmed. It seemed like I was being directed to think and act in ways that did not bring about the best kinds of thoughts. I'm not saying that all the things that I felt or sensed were bad.

"My thoughts are a direct result of the kind of information going into my head."

I am just making it clear that <u>I could sense influence in my psyche when listening, versus not listening to the constant streams of information from these various entertainment devices.</u> Sometimes, I would begin to act a bit strange after soaking up stimulation my entertainment devices for a few hours non-stop!

The second factor: I concluded was that frequent repetitive use of the TV, radio, and music was blocking me from hearing my inner voice. We all have an inner voice that is continually attempting to speak to us. However, because there is so much "noise" being dumped into our brains, it is nearly impossible to hear what that voice is saying with the "noise" regularly streaming in.

The third conclusion: I had <u>unknowingly</u> given control over for the programming of my mind over to the devices, music, shows, and television. It was my constant use of them that had allowed the encoding of my brain with useless, negative-garbage information and programs that drove my thoughts in a direction that did not help me.

The information I was receiving DID NOT help me in becoming a better person. It did not further my career! It served no useful purpose that helped me to stop being a jerk to my girlfriends during those times!

I was unconscious and inattentive to this detrimental subconscious programming. Sadly, most of us have been programmed our entire lives in this way. We have given the power of programming of what goes into our brain, over to outside forces, and we never gave it a second thought when doing so.

This classic repeated, unconscious and inattentive subconscious programming of our brain, which we allowed to happen is a massive part of what makes us who we are. It seems as though, we are always plugged into some kind of electronic device that I firmly believe distracts us from hearing our inner voice. When I was at home, it was the TV. When I was in the car, it is the radio.

Whenever I worked out, it was music/radio! At work or in between, it is Facebook and Instagram. Even when sitting on the toilet, I had my cell phone! Crazy!

<u>Part of How to Be a Better Dude and Treat Your Lady Right is that you MUST get in touch with yourself and hear your inner voice. You MUST start to de-program yourself a bit from old ways of thinking and being.</u>

You already know that the way you are acting right now isn't working. So, IF you want to keep your Precious Lady at your side, then the changes need to happen now!

"I am succeeding in my personal growth journey every day."

I will never tell anyone to do what I did as far as cutting back, but I want you to understand — **I was VERY much corrupted in thoughts, actions, and behaviors.** So, I had some incredibly intense levels of ugliness to eliminate from the depths of my heart.

I found so much freedom when I started to direct my thinking with this new version of me, instead of letting the old me dominating the scene. I was polluted, toxic, volatile, and angry. I would say that I had a hair-triggered "kick your a** attitude!"

The truth is that I had to accept the fact that I was a by-product of everything that I had been exposed to all these years. **TV and radio were not my friends!**

Again, let me emphasize. I will not tell you to entirely stop listening or watching all of those forms of entertainment of which you currently are tied to. However, if you find yourself watching reality shows depicting deception, lies, jealousy, back-stabbing, revenge and infidelity, then you may want to question how your mind is being shaped.

If you listen to the radio or music that degrades and trashes women, then you may want to consider putting yourself on a large-scale reduction of it.

"Garbage In = Garbage Out."

If you want to be a better man, then you need high-quality information going into your brain.

You MUST take charge and assume the role of the "Master Programmer" and direct what gets into your brain! Keep in mind that we are all the result of information that has been taken in and stored by our subconscious mind.

Ninety percent of All of our conscious thoughts come from the subconscious mind. The subconscious mind records EVERYTHING and brings it to the surface of your conscious thoughts. The most Dominant Mental Operating Programs are what make you who you are.

"My Precious Lady sees a New Man in front of her who is loving and kind."

If you want to improve almost anything about yourself or learn a new skill, talent or ability, it has been shown that repeated exposure to that particular task of interest, your brain will activate your brain's neurons and create a new communication center (Neural-Network). This too assists you in the mastery of that specific task or area of interest. Keep in mind that it does not matter whether the mission is good or bad; the bottom-line is that repeated exposure develops the Neural-Network.

Initially, many people will scoff at the mention that the regular use of entertainment devices, music and TV productions can impact one's thinking negatively. I can certainly understand why they reject it because I used to be in that camp also. **I was a DJ in college. So, my natural inclination was to dismiss it all as bogus BS of the highest order.**

What dramatically and convincingly changed my mind is that it came down to learning how the brain works! Learning about, *"Why did I think a certain way?"*

Why did I react the way that I do? Why did I have these impulse flashes of irritation? Why was I bitter? Why did I curse and swear at my girlfriend, and call her names? I wanted answers! The million-dollar question is, do you?

Do you want to fix the problem? Assuming you do, then start the process with the information in this study-guide book.

Without proper knowledge or new information going into your head, you are doomed to repeat the same old negative, self-destructive-relationship destroying habits that have dominated you up to this point. I had unknowingly allowed a lot of mental damage to occur to me.

One day, I woke up and said NO MORE!

Today, I am the Master Programmer. I have transformed who I was. As a result, I became a better person for my Special Lady, my children, my friends, my co-workers and for society! **You as well can make the most incredible and spectacular transformation into becoming the *New You*!**

"Every day I put good information into my brain, and this produces good thoughts."

CHAPTER 6

21 Years Old Chronologically, But Acting 10 Years Old Emotionally!

Sure, you may be 21 years old and well-beyond in terms of your age. However, I personally think that it is a most excellent thing to be doing regardless of your age. As our laws would have it, at 21 years of life, you are considered a "full-fledged adult male." Basically, society calls you a "man." Chronologically you may be 21, are 25, 38, 45, or even 60 years of age **but is a number of 21 years of age and even beyond, all that it takes to achieve manhood?**

I submit to you, absolutely not!! Let me be all together clear, just because you are 21 years of age or older, or even much older, this alone should not be the only qualifier for any of us claiming manhood!

Let me clarify where I am going with this. If you are one of those guys, who call yourself a man, and your way of living is to rough up your Special Lady mentally or physically, I say NO WAY! Many men regularly verbally abuse their Precious Lady with venomous speech, thoughtless actions or behaviors that destroy a woman's mental and emotional state of mind. You are not a "Real Man" in my personal opinion!

Sure, I will agree that you have the years on earth that give you legal status in our society as a man. **However, here is the real question; If you carry on with your emotions to where you berate, bully and verbally abuse your lady, how old do you really think you are "emotionally?"**

I understand that you may not like what I am saying here. When I first heard this kind of information years ago, I flipped out and rejected nearly all of it. What saved me was that I did some intense self-reflection. I got sincerely honest with myself. Once I did, I immediately went to work on improving myself. I strongly encourage you to do the same.

Be real about how you act and how you think!

Below are a few questions that should provide you valuable insight into where you are emotionally. Honesty is always your best friend. Don't run from it. Run to it and embrace the truth and it will turn your life around in unimaginably positive ways.

"In the morning, I greet my love with a smile and joy."

If you find yourself described in any one of these listed behaviors, then count yourself as acting very immature emotionally!

- *Do you rant and rave at your lady to ensure that you break her down emotionally until she cries?*

- *Do you think that your verbal assaults, volleys of brutalizing language and belittlement are what a man does to his Special Lady?*

- *Do you go out and party, drink your beer, and run with the boys, — only to come home in the late night in a drunken stupor, looking for hot sexual interaction with your lady?*

Let's Get This Straight: Emotionally, some of you are still acting like young boys. The truth is that it comes down to managing your temperament and how you view who is supposed to be your greatest gift in your life (your woman).

Your emotions fly out of control whenever you get upset with her about a multitude of things. You start cursing, screaming, throwing objects, breaking things, taking rings back, revenge tactics, and deliberately crushing the tender heart of your Special Lady! Whoa! This has got to stop, or you will lose her permanently!

I know many men who are age 30, 40 or 50 years old. They whine like a baby and claim to be a victim! They consistently use the "shield of justification" for their out of control state of existence!

In my experience, and it is also the view of every woman who I have ever known, this kind of insensitive and thoughtless behavior is quite barbaric. It is utterly demeaning to the woman with whom you claim to love so much!

I have not met a woman who likes it when a man yells at her nor does she enjoy being threatened, degraded and emotionally trampled! *Hmmm, I wonder why that is?*

"I always treat my precious lady well in all circumstances of life."

Some men will claim that they did not know that their behavior was really that bad or that it seemed like it was NOT that big of a deal. The reason why one can reach that conclusion is due to the number of years of living **Unconsciously Unaware**.

A more straightforward way of saying it is that you turned a blind eye to your negative thinking and behaviors. You grew comfortable in being this way. Hey, we ALL are guilty of getting comfortable with bad habits and actions! This is our way of removing guilt. We think that we are okay just the way we are. I can easily relate! However, you know in your gut, just the same way that I knew, that I had to do something to be better. I am not doing the right thing in treating my lady in a mean, hurtful and cruel way.

If you know that your relationship is in trouble and it is because you acted like a thoughtless, and insensitive bastard at times, then you MUST make immediate corrective actions to your behavior. *Start today!*

What A Real Man Does Not Do to His Woman. EVER!

A "Real Man" DOES NOT verbally, physically or emotionally abuse his most cherished Special Lady under any set of circumstances. <u>Your lady should ALWAYS be held in the highest regard. You should be the one to protect her from the harsh treatment of the world in which we live!</u>

She should NEVER have to fear you or the crudeness of your heart, behaviors, and actions! Ask yourself: **"Do you agree, with that?"** I hope so, my friend!

How do you say that you love her, yet you blurt out tirades of scandalous insults that obliterate her emotionally, and then, you continue to treat her like trash?

I am very curious to know how you can think that you qualify as a man? What am I seriously wondering is if you even qualify to count yourself as someone who belongs to a fair, just and kind society?

Sure, you may think I'm a bit harsh, but I know that some of you have heads as thick as mine. You need the pressure put on yourself to shake you up a bit. It wakes you from your state of living <u>Unconsciously Unaware</u>.

"I compliment and praise my Lovely Lady every day."

Why Am I So Tough on Those Who Call Themselves Men?

This is because, I have seen the ugly results of such behavior, as well as the emotional trauma and scarring inflicted on a woman! I used to be right there with you AND thought that I was right for being that way. I was DEAD WRONG! Man, I was so blind and so ignorant for so many years!

So, consider this training guide as my way of being part of the solution to the problem. Make a stand to assist those men who would like to make a change to stop the cruelty, and the repeated psychological destructive behaviors against their most Precious and Lovely Lady.

I am a hardliner about what I am saying because I believe that women should always be treated with loving kindness at all times!

There appears to be a rampant problem all around the world. We, as men, make up all kinds of reasons and excuses as to why we are treating our women so poorly. Many times, the excuses are: "I don't know, I just didn't feel good! She knows that I really didn't mean it." Or, "I had a really bad day."

If you are acting out in this way or similar, then let me say ANY verbal speech said with a nasty or mean tone is a fierce and thoughtless assault on her emotional well-being! **STOP IT!**

It is a sad day in the world when a man *thinks* he is a man, yet he treats his Lovely Lady worse than sewer waste by-product!

The truth is that it takes work to be a "Real Man." You must consistently and persistently work at it. You must infuse new information into the gray matter of your emotionally under-performing brain!

Stop Making Excuses! Stop the Rationalizations!

Stop ALL THE CRAP WITH ANY ABUSIVE BEHAVIOR!

Quit lying to yourself and realize that you must make a stand. You are going to be a far better man from this moment forward!

"This is a new beginning for both me and our relationship – I am a New Man."

I have two huge questions for you:

- ***Are you going to be a "Real Man?"***
- ***Are you willing to do what it takes to become that man?***

Your Special Lady is waiting for you to make the right decision.

It's up to you to put an end to the deep pain she is in!

Here is the final outcome of all of my research. This is what I believe you should be doing from this point forward.

Take it upon yourself to learn about what your lady likes. What does she desire in you and from you? You can start by understanding that she will love it when you hold her and speak to her gently, warmly speaking with words of love and tenderness. Starting today, hold her close and speak from your heart! Communicate with intense passion, heat and a raging firestorm of love! Tell her what you adore about her and how much she means to you.

Understand This: Women cannot give the kind of love and devotion that they are capable of until they are free to do so! They can only do this in a state of mind that allows them to be relaxed, and to exist around you with zero fear! IF your woman has a fear of you, and that you may go off the deep end about something, then it is up to you to change this starting today.

Let this sink in for a moment, over the years, you have developed and magnified a bad habit. That habit CAN be broken! You CAN replace the bad habits with outstanding new habits that shine a light of love, joy, and happiness upon the Special Lady of Your Life!

If you emotionally act like a 10-year-old boy, then it is incredibly hard for a woman ever to get excited about that. They live in fear of your next temper tantrum.

"I speak words that lift the spirit and the heart of my sweet loving lady."

Do You Love Your Woman and Want Her to Stay by your Side?

IF you love your lady and you want to be the best man for her ever, then you must fully embrace all that I share with you in this manual.

If you are willing to continue reading this information and make a masterful effort to practice the mental exercises and readily repeat the steps, then you will find that a *New You* will begin to arise! You will FEEL IT!

Rewire Your Brain and Here is What Can Happen:

- You CAN crush and destroy the *old you*.
- You CAN eliminate negative, and demeaning speech!
- You CAN get rid of malice actions and revengeful thoughts!
- You CAN blow away flash-anger and hurtful speech!
- You CAN stop cold the emotional abuse tone and language!
- You CAN lift her up and praise her, increasing her self-worth!
- You CAN become a better man at the speed of your thoughts!

ALL OF THESE, and so much more, are possible when you start the transformative process of becoming a New and Improved Man — a man who uses his tongue and actions to build up and not tear down!

You MUST make a stand to begin the process, starting right at this moment. You do that by continuing to read and apply what you are learning!

"I am dedicated to the efforts that will assist me in healing my lady's heart."

CHAPTER 7

Are You Guilty of Emotionally Destroying Your Lady?

"What You Do Speaks So Loudly That I Cannot Hear What You Say!"

Okay guys, some of you may think that I'm a bit hard on you, but just consider it tough love. I am not here to bash us or put us down. I am merely attempting to express the severity of the problem of which we are faced with.

My points are these:

- You said that you are really in love with her!
- You said that you need her and want her!
- You said that she is the love of your life!
- You said that you could not live without her!
- You said that you would do anything for her!
- You said that no one could compare to her!
- You said she is the best lady in your life ever!
- You said that you would never hurt her!

Well, let me ask you this most important question. Most of you who are reading this already know that you have been moody, insensitive, uncaring, unpredictably irritable, temperamental and — at times — down-right hard on your Special and Most Precious Lady.

If you say that you care for her so much, and your love is so deep for her, then why do you continue to do these things and worse? This is a cruel type of behavior!

"If my mood is off, I STILL smile and give loving attention to my Special Love."

How many times have you called your Lovely Lady vulgarities such as:

- B_tch
- Slut
- Stupid
- C_nt
- Piece of Sh_t
- F_ckin' b_tch
- Dumb a_s
- A_sh_le
- Idiot

WARNING
Graphic Content:
VIEWER DISCRETION ADVISED

I will tell you right now that if you are guilty of any of this, then you need to STOP RIGHT NOW with these kinds of actions!

These words are brutally cruel and insensitive and are damaging the heart and mind of your Precious Lady!

A "Real Man" would NEVER say these things to his most loved and precious gift from God above!

Right now, a great sadness is weighing heavy on my soul. I know that today across the world, many women will be brutalized under a barrage of verbal self-image crippling assaults! Worst yet, some will even be physically harmed. This is the highly destructive process of tearing down a woman emotionally.

And, if you are one of those guys who do this, I implore you to STOP! Think!

What in the hell are we doing? What are we thinking? What is this vile, incendiary vitriol that we rapid-fire from our mouths with laser-beam precision to the heart and mind of the woman that we supposedly love?

Question for You: **What definition of love do you know that allows for the insidious and vicious acts of verbally beating the life out of a woman?** What kind of love is this? Buddy, if you think this type of behavior is love, then you have a serious problem!

"If my mood is off, I STILL smile and give loving attention to my Special Love."

Emotional and mental abuse in the United States is running rampant! **Emotional abuse is an evil and destructive force, that is inflicted on thousands of women every day by the very men who "SAID" that they love them!!!**

There is no known description of love that allows for the onslaught of such hateful, mean, spiteful and barbaric language to be used, as a destructive force on the emotions of the "Love of Your Life!"

Her heart, words, and pain are asking you- STOP NOW!

"If I am tired, I STILL speak to my lovely lady with beautiful words of love."

I am amazed that we can live in a world where so many songs and TV shows glorify love, but we still have such incredibly high numbers of abuse on women. So, why is it that men are so abusive to the one that they love? <u>If this applies to you, then you have to ask yourself some very critical questions. What is inside of your heart that causes you to be ruthless at times to the most precious person in your life?</u> No matter what your reasons or excuses are, this study-guide book, IF applied vigorously, CAN be a powerful life-changing tool to assist you in breaking the cycle of your emotionally destructive actions on your Lovely Lady.

You Don't Have to Hit to Hurt!

Your words can carry much power, and you can easily deeply traumatize and scar your Precious Lady for the rest of her life with your cruel and heartless verbal assaults.

Violence is Not Just Physical!

If this is a part of your life, you need to end it right away and never ever go down this road again. Think Man! You would not feel so good at all if someone carried out those same verbally aggressive actions on you!

STOP the Emotional Abuse!

The truth is that none of us like to be yelled at, and called horribly repulsive and **100%** inexcusable names under any condition! **STOP THE ABUSE NOW!**

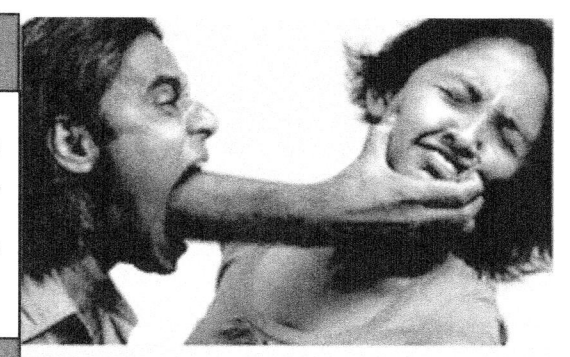

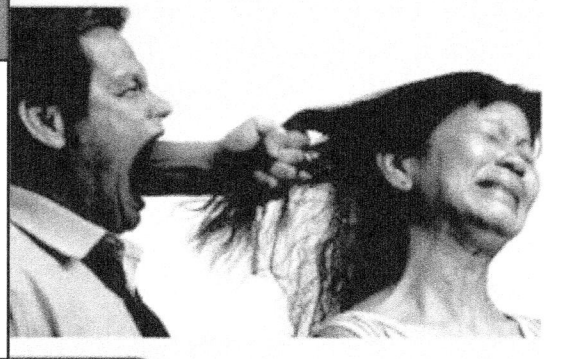

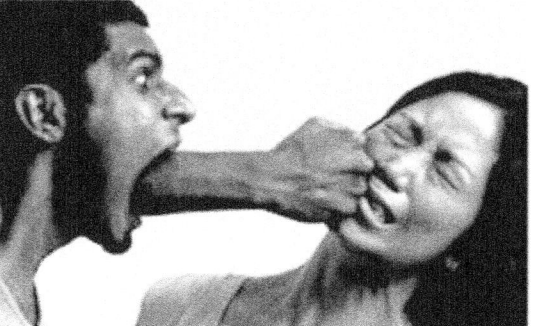

"My words are loving, beautiful and enriching to the heart and mind of my Precious Lady."

Every Year, there are TENS of THOUSANDS of women who are emotionally abused by the man who supposedly loves them! Of course, the man will claim that he is going to change. Real change can only happen, though, with a change in thoughts. New thoughts are the result of New Information. This, my friend, is what this study guide book is all about!

So, what do you think is going on in the heart and mind of a man that makes this kind of behavior his way of being? The answer lies in the way that one "thinks!" Dominant Mental Operating Programs are laid down in the very foundation of who he is, and over time those programs give rise to the beast, who thrives on breaking the will of a beautiful woman!

These kinds of ugly thoughts give way to harsh words that are spoken. Then come dominating and threatening actions. When these thoughts and actions are repeated enough, they eventually lead to a highly specialized Neural-Network in your brain that is "hair-trigger." It is ready to carry out a blistering, lightning fast reaction loaded with hate, evil and appalling words and actions. When this process is repeatedly performed it most likely, will become a well-entrenched harmful habit!

This kind of reaction is a "LEARNED" behavior. The degrading treatment is "LEARNED." The ugly and malicious verbal beat-downs are "LEARNED." This kind of vicious behavior and wicked treatment of a woman is "LEARNED."

As a statement of fact, I emphasize throughout this study-guide book, your brain is wired in such a way to help you learn things with an extremely high degree of efficiency. Once you continually go forth with repeating almost any action consistently, whether that action is good or bad, your brain will begin to naturally wire in the process.

"I will always treat my precious lady well in all circumstances of life."

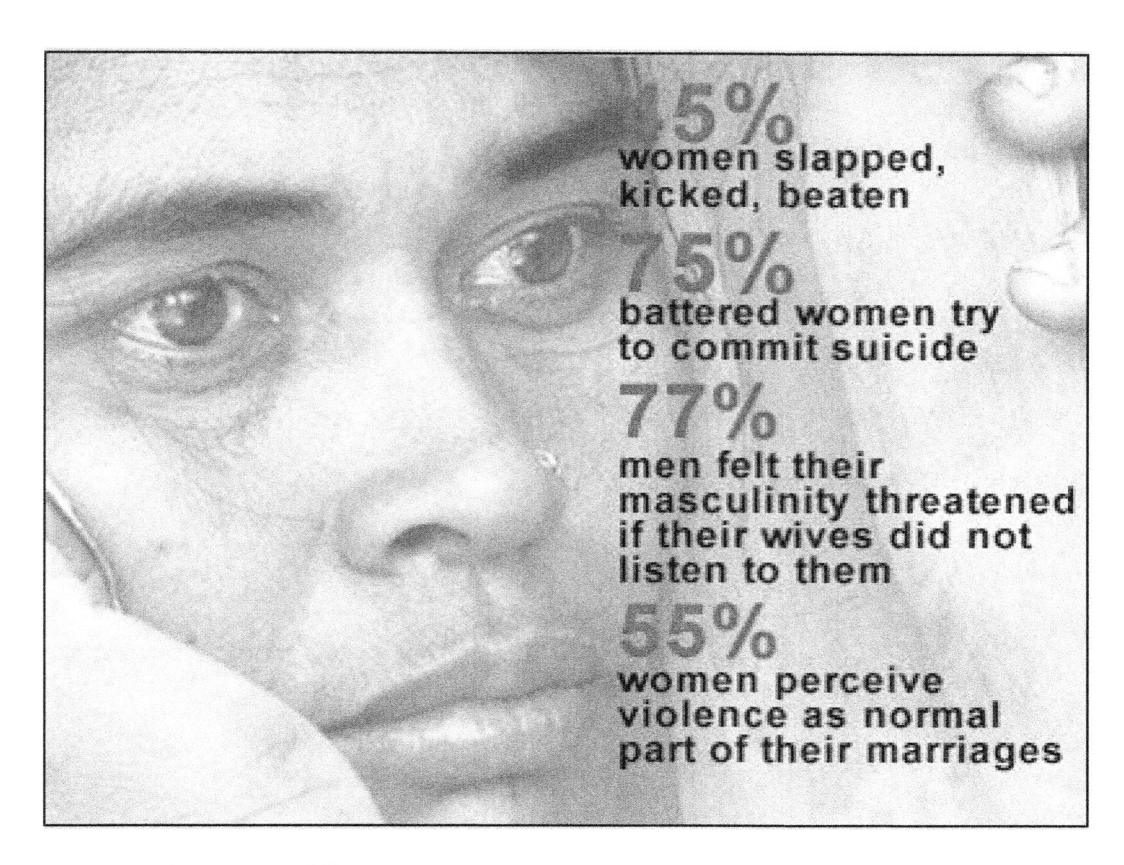

5% women slapped, kicked, beaten

75% battered women try to commit suicide

77% men felt their masculinity threatened if their wives did not listen to them

55% women perceive violence as normal part of their marriages

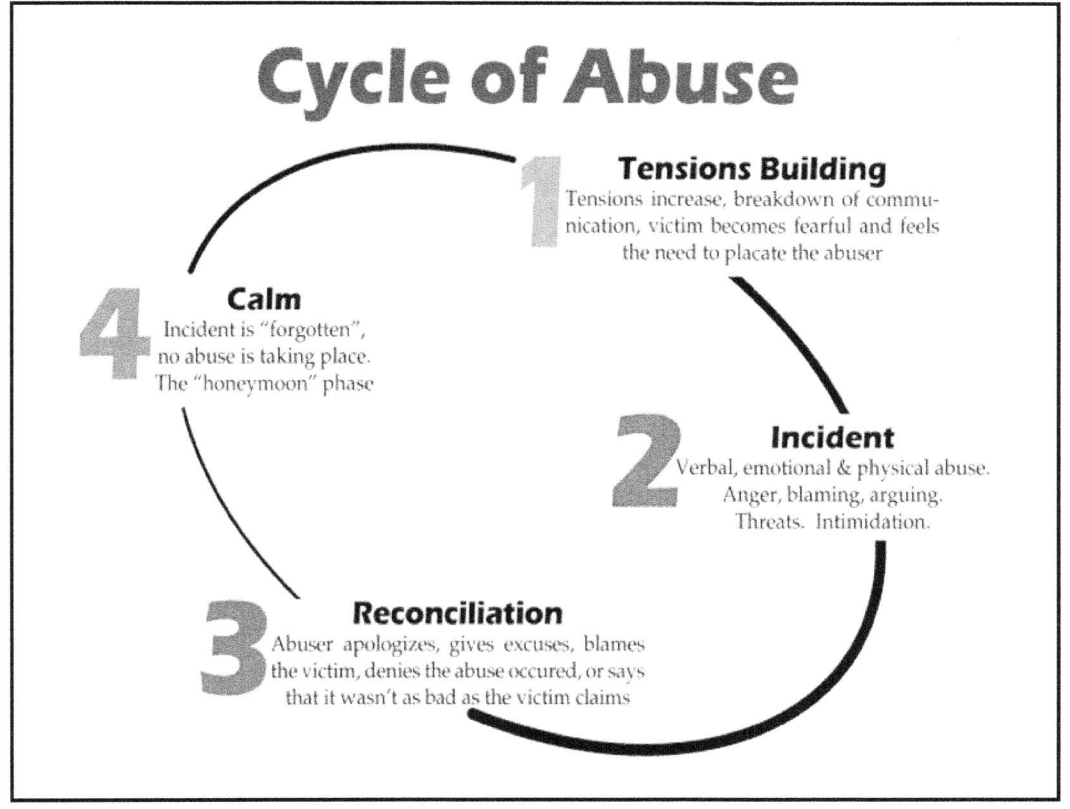

Cycle of Abuse

1. Tensions Building
Tensions increase, breakdown of communication, victim becomes fearful and feels the need to placate the abuser

2. Incident
Verbal, emotional & physical abuse. Anger, blaming, arguing. Threats. Intimidation.

3. Reconciliation
Abuser apologizes, gives excuses, blames the victim, denies the abuse occured, or says that it wasn't as bad as the victim claims

4. Calm
Incident is "forgotten", no abuse is taking place. The "honeymoon" phase

"I relate to my Beautiful Lady with only words that are soft, gentle, praise and love."

So, if you are guilty of any kind of abuse and you want to save your relationship with your awesome lady, then I recommend that you look in the mirror and make the commitment to yourself. Take the necessary actions needed to STOP NOW!

IF you are one, who abuses on any level or feels that you are on the edge of doing so, please start with these Neuron Activation Builder Scripts right away! Train Hard!

- Repeat this regularly throughout the day.
- Just read it in your mind the first few days.
- On the third day: Say it out loud and with emotion.

For Added Effect:

- grab a photo of your Lady
- look in the mirror at yourself
- speak with verbal strength
- bring forth strong emotion
- visualize yourself as a New Man

I cannot emphasize how important these Mental Brain Exercises are to your personal development. Guys, get it into your head!

When you regularly and repeatedly have a strong desire, and intense emotion do these exercises, then you give your brain the power to rewire itself.

Your brain naturally likes to learn, so, if you expose it to a stimulus, often enough your brain Neurons are activated that assist in establishing new patterns of thought and actions. Just consider it a way of self-programming yourself to wash out the old ways of thinking and doing while bringing in the new ways of thinking and doing.

"My words are loving, beautiful and enriching to the heart and mind of my Precious Lady."

My Thoughts and Words are Positive, Fresh…

New Man Mind Trainer # 2

My thoughts and words are positive, fresh and filled with love and admiration for my Precious Lady. I am a New Man and every morning, I come to _____, with a smile, a hug and a kiss to express my feelings of warmth and love. I have taken full repsonsiblity for all of my actions, and bring forth ONLY kind, and gentle actions towards the great love of my life.

When I speak to _____, she will hear words that build her up because my mouth flows with positive energy that heals her heart. I speak words EVERY DAY that compliment her and praise her.

My old ways are GONE! I am a New Man! I have a New and Better Mind and thus all of thoughts and actions flow with kindness, gentleness, patience and love. *(end of affirmation)*

Yes, your own words read and spoken out loud to yourself have the power to rewire your brain. They give rise to new, good, positive and healthy relationship thoughts. *(Desire, Emotion, and Repetition are the key)*

When I Begin My Day, I am Focused

New Man Mind Trainer # 3

When I start my day, I am focused on reaching out with a gentle heart of loving passion to my Lovely lady and greet her with a smile and warm embrace. With a warm heart I express to her with my words and actions how much she means to me. I do this because I am a New Man and I am a man who always treats his Precious Lady like a Princess. I have abandoned my old ways of being! I read positive information EVERY DAY. I am thoughtful, sensitive and caring for the needs and desires of my lady.

I love _____, so deeply and richly and that is shown by the words that I speak to her and all of my actions towards her. *(end of affirmation)*

"I now CHOOSE a New Way of being, and ALL of my actions show I am a New Man."

I am a Transformed Man

New Man Mind Trainer # 4

I am a Transformed Man, who talks and walks in a light of goodness to all who I encounter in my day. In God's Word it says, "As I think in my heart, so am I" --- Well then, I am flexible, patient, giving, abundantly loving and filled with positive energy in every aspect of my daily living. I choose to be a man who loves his lady with the best of who I am every day. She deserves a good man, and that good man is ME.

I think with clear thoughts for ALWAYS doing the right and fair action. I think with a heart of showing love to my Special Lady. My words to _____, are new, inspiring and breathes new life and love into our relationship. She is my world and I appreciate the love she has shown me, and thus, I treat her as my special gift from God above. I am a Transformed Man. I am a Better Man and I passionately embrace all of these wonderful new attitudes that are now a part of who I am. *(end of affirmation)*

Yes, your own words read and spoken out loud to yourself have the power to rewire your brain and give rise to new, good, positive and healthy relationship thoughts. *(Desire, Emotion, and Repetition are the key)*

As I Wake Up This Morning

New Man Mind Trainer # 5

As I wake up this morning, my mind is filled with thoughts of how I can satisfy and please my Precious Love with new creative actions. I will give to her words that show how great my love is for her. I will speak of how fantastic I think that she is. I will speak to her with words that reflect my dedication and devotion to her.

_____, will hear a new, different, and better side of me when I speak to her. I cherish and adore my Lovely Lady. She completes me in a multitude of ways and causes my heart to soar. So, on this day, with God as my witness, I will hold her close and speak my heart to her, and ALL of my actions will reflect the words that I now speak.

I am a New Man, and I speak as a New Man and my actions are that of a New Man.

(end of affirmation)

"From the time I wake-up, until I go to bed, I work to improve myself as a New Man."

As a wrap-up on this chapter, I want to stress that if you're going to change something about yourself that is negative or embrace a new positive trait, then it is entirely possible to do so. You must commit to positive action steps that help you to build the mental resources that you will need to have permanent change.

Don't fall into the age-old trap that says, you cannot change.

That is an Outright LIE!

Do what is outlined in the book and you will be blown away by how you can feel change surging through you. Also, whether you believe in God or not, just drop to your knees sometimes, and pray for insight, wisdom and the power to change. Staying consistent in your new efforts, paired up with a strong desire and unyielding belief, within a day or two, you will start to feel the power of a revolution will unfolding inside of you!

As for the New Man's Mind Trainer Scripts: You can always modify them to suit your particular situation if you need something more specific. The critical thing to keep in mind is to remember to write and speak them positively with your thoughts projecting that you are already where you want to be. **DO NOT focus on old broken personality traits and habits**. Speak and write in the present tense that you "already are" or "you already have" whatever change it is that you desire.

Quick example: I would say, "I am a new man," not – "I am going to be a new man."

Quick example: I would say, "I am positive and uplifting," not – "I am going to be."

Affirmations are spoken as though you already have whatever it is you want.

There is no need to speak on what or how you used to be. The *old you* is to be considered dead to your new journey of personal growth and development.

"I CHOOSE my attitudes and moods, and they are positive, good and uplifting."

Here is a little more of an explanation on the best way to create and speak your affirmations.

Example: Long before I really was a "New Man" --- I spoke those words long before I was a "New Man," and I did this every day. I would constantly visualize myself as that New Man every day. These kinds of actions establish a new attitude within yourself QUICKLY!

I didn't say, "**I will be**." Rather, I would say: "**I am.**" I would rarely focus on the negative behavior by making statements such as, "I will not curse anymore" or "I will not yell anymore." Instead, 98% of the time, I will put the focus on what positive trait, action or habit that I wanted as my change.

I would write and speak as though I already had what I wanted. I would speak it with positive words, such as "I only speak with clean and healthy words" or "I speak softly and gently to my lady at all times."

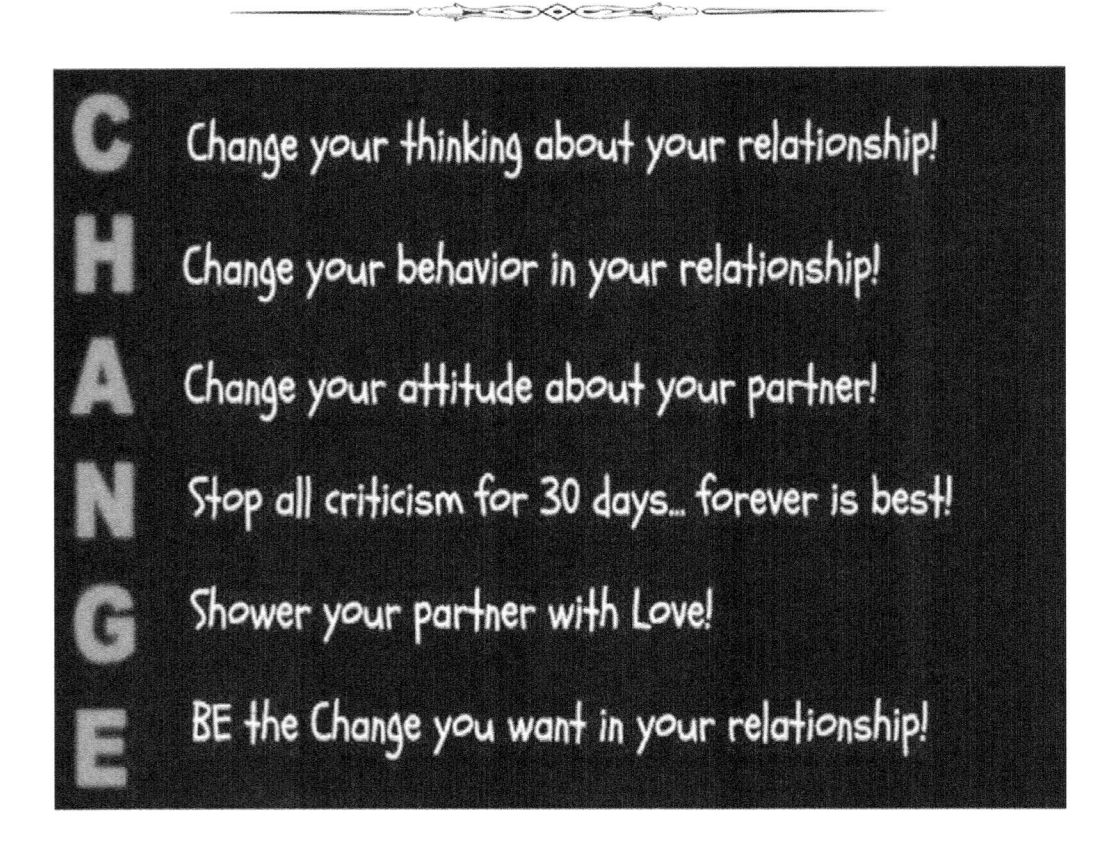

CHANGE

- **C** — Change your thinking about your relationship!
- **H** — Change your behavior in your relationship!
- **A** — Change your attitude about your partner!
- **N** — Stop all criticism for 30 days... forever is best!
- **G** — Shower your partner with Love!
- **E** — BE the Change you want in your relationship!

"I build-up my Lovely Lady and my attitude towards her is ALWAYS kind and loving."

Chapter 8

Love's Potent Silent Killers

Ignore and Neglect

Are you one of those men who ignore their Lovely Lady, and rarely engage her in conversation? If so, shame on you!

Some of you will say, "But I did not know that I was ignoring her!" Well, even if you did not know, that tells me that you are not paying attention to your actions and communications in your relationship. No excuses my friend, for you should already know this.

Over the years, I have heard some of the craziest excuses that can be manufactured by men to deflect the blame for the actions of ignoring and neglecting their Lovely Lady.

Truth Be Told: You are just going to have to suck it up, as I slap you upside your head again. These thoughtless acts cause the pain and devastation that you are creating within your lady!

The reality of the matter is that your reasons are INEXCUSABLE! You know EXACTLY what in the heck you are doing! You are not entirely blind to your own actions, and now you can see how sad she seems these days. You know that something is wrong.

If you have a lady that you have neglected for any reason, **you have failed miserably at meeting her most basic emotional needs.**

The real story behind here is that this is just another sad habit of which you fell into or it is something that you never learned how to do your entire life. Either way, it is something that you can immediately begin to improve. However, you must first have some empathy and insight on how neglecting her causes her to feel.

"I instantly apologize for any errors in behavior that I may display. Instantly!!!!"

A Woman Should NEVER Be Ignored or Neglected for ANY REASON!

I do not give a crap about your job and stress! Nor do I care if your meeting with the president of the United States is not going so well. **If you repeatedly ignore your most precious lady, then you have committed a crime of "Death to Her Soul."**

She has relied on you! She has admired you and trusted you! She has supported you and believed in you! Now you have taken it upon yourself, to let her be without your devoted love and attention.

YOUR direct and indirect actions have created an environment to where her world feels icy cold, desolate and empty. Trust me on this; **she feels abandoned by you!**

In this cold, dark and lonely world, she has reached out to you so many times saying, "*Help me*" by her actions and sometimes her inactions. Yes, your most Precious Love has expressed to you countless times through her words, actions and behaviors. *"What does she need to do to earn your attention?"*

She gives you both verbal and non-verbal cues and clues. Still, you remain hardcore deaf, dumb and blind in acknowledging that very sad and highly disappointed look on her face.

She pleads with you to please not leave her this way!!! Her further actions strongly communicate that she needs you, and the outward expressions of your love! But, because you have been so busy with life (the boys, the job, the club, the soccer league, the business, the dogs, the kids or whatever, you have left her to feel worthless, empty, cold and isolated from you and your feelings for her.

Is this what being a man is all about? **HELL NO!!**

Listen up, my friend! You are bleeding the life out of your woman, through the constant bombardment of the ruthless silent killers called "ignore and neglect!"

If it has not already happened, then she will find comfort in the arms of someone else. This action on her behalf, though wrong, is an effort to feel loved and wanted! Once that happens, you will feel like a major piece of crap!

"I shower my Precious Lady with many tender moments of loving affection."

You Need to Get to Work Immediately and Reverse the Damage of the Silent Killers of Ignoring and Neglect

You need to go to her IMMEDIATELY and confess that you have been a colossal bonehead!!! Do everything in your power to let her know that you indeed are sorry and that you clearly see what you have been doing.

Man-up and then you can become a "Real Man."

When was the last time that you stepped up, took her by the hand, and walked with her? When was the last time that you made it a point to tell her how she is your "Princess or the Bright Shining Star of Your Life?"

When was the last time you slowed down in your fast-paced life to surprise her with words and actions that made her heart and soul soar to the heavens?

You know it, and I know it! You know that it is totally and completely wrong and that there is no justification on earth that can excuse it!

News Flash: **If your relationship has been ugly and negative for quite a while, then she may have already walked away emotionally!**

<u>Maybe all of this is her fault?</u> So, if she is that bad of woman why are you still there trying to have a relationship with someone who does not want to be in a relationship with you? Staying in such an environment is not suitable for either of you! **Make A Decision!**

Man-up! Make the decision to treat each other right! **It starts with YOU!** I will presume because you are reading this book, you obviously want it to work out; *Does she?*

<u>**You Be the "Man" and "Lead**</u>!!!" **Lead with Love!** Remake yourself and be transformed into a man that any woman would be proud to know and boast about!

You **have the ability** to change, grow and even transform with the power of choice! Choose to grow and become more than you ever thought possible! It is within your control, and you can start TODAY! Just make the decision!

It should be self-evident that fighting with your lady and arguing every day over ridiculous things has no place in your life!

"IF I had a tough day at work, I STILL greet my lady with abundant kisses and love."

A relationship should not be based on ego, power or might!

In fact, when working together, solutions that either person could contribute to solving matters of importance, could work out — just as long as the couple embraced the suggested solutions with enthusiasm and a willingness to have success.

A healthy relationship should utilize what is known as a "shared team success strategy." It supports the idea that BOTH of you get behind potential solutions and back them with high optimism and a solution-oriented mindset regardless of who came up with the idea. The suggested solution or idea, regardless of who came up with it is given full effort from both parties to make it work. There is no concern about who will be right in the end because when you both work together to find fair, equitable and reasonable solutions, then you both win in the end. You both are right!

Both of you should be striving towards being highly-flexible and highly-adaptable when working together on anything for a solution. Both of your attitudes should be light and easy, and don't be afraid to throw some humor around. *Way to go, TEAM!*

LISTEN to what your lady is saying to you. This is what I have learned in all decision-making situations. Many times, she will see things from a different perspective than you do. Additionally, many women seem to have a very natural, intuitive energy within them.

Whenever she sees things from a different angle, you should embrace it as a good thing and not a bad thing! IF you change your attitude and LISTEN, you will find that her voice in all matters can be wise, helpful and insightful!

Guys, believe me; listening to your lady is a brilliant idea! Many women seem to have an almost like a "sixth sense" that can guide you better in ALL facets of your life!

So, why in the world are you arguing with her? Why are you telling her that her suggestions, recommendations, and ideas are stupid or won't work?

Change the way that you are viewing her. Embrace her for the intelligent and very astute person that she is and LISTEN!

This is a definitive plan of action that you can implement right now!

"I am insightful about what she wants, interests & needs may be, and I respond quickly."

How to Be a Better Dude and Treat Your Lady Right

> **As a New Man, I AM Thoughtful and Kind**
>
> **New Man Mind Trainer # 6**
>
> As a New Man, I AM thoughtful and kind in all discussions of ANY type. I will listen closely to my lady's concern and work to be insightful to what she is communicating to me. I will have a heart of empathy and understanding at all times.
>
> In mind, I am already thinking about her needs and how I can so easily give her moments of tenderness, caring and warmth. I automatically reach out to hold her, touch her and show her how much that I love her.
>
> I am a New Man who can think, speak and act in ways that bring great physical expression of comfort to my lovely lady. *(end of affirmation)*

"IF I had a tough day at work, I STILL greet my lady with abundant kisses and love."

Chapter 9

What? No Physical Affection for Your Lady!

You Give Her Virtually Zero Non-Sexual Communication

No touching, no cuddling, no holding, no stroking her face, no caressing her arms, and no pulling her close! *Are you smoking crack?*

Here is what your physical actions towards her are saying: "*I only want to touch you when we are having sex!*" AND: "*If it were possible to have sex with you without holding on to you, then I would really like that!*"

But wait, there's more! What makes this worst, is that you expect her to be a hot, motivated sex machine for you on demand! Yep, you know what I mean regarding this matter exactly.

You have, with surgical precision, removed physical embracing or romantic gestures from your relationship. In fact, in your mind, you feel like everything is okay, or even good! Let me set the record straight. If you are one of these guys, then you are shooting yourself in your own foot — with a 12-gauge shotgun!

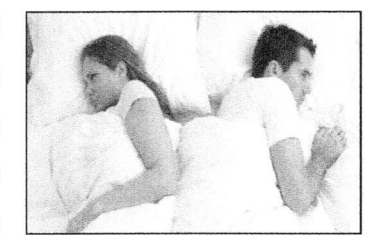

Men, Please Note: Women love to be held in a non-sexual way at times. They love to be held close and told how important they are to you.

For those times, when you have finished with sexual interludes of heated passion, a woman loves to be cuddled, verbally bathed and lathered with your words of love and the soft caring strokes of your fingers on her face. **When was the last time that you did that?** You think you know what you are doing?

You think that you are some kind of "Don Juan," but you lack the most basic skills in winning the heart of a woman!

Did you know that many women feel the most secure with you in the relationship when they can snuggle right up next to you while watching a movie or TV? You reassure them with moments of touching, caressing and holding. By the way, this is not the time she is seeking sex from you; she just wants your closeness, tenderness and your dedicated attention to surrounding her with your love.

"Today, I celebrate the joy of my Lovely Lady with a special note or text to her"

If you are the guy who thinks that this kind of attention means she wants sexual fulfillment, then you should consider revamping your thinking, and your approach to your woman needs immediately. *Chances are very high that it is not the time for sex.*

It is time to move past your single-mindedness of desires. Make things happen for her just by taking the initiative and giving her conversation about love and presenting non-sexual physical attention.

Here are some things that you can act on immediately!

They go something like this:

- **I will do something awesome for her right now; that is simple.**
- **I will go ahead and stroke her hair with my fingers right now.**
- **I will whisper sweet words of love and goodness into her ear.**
- **Let me hold her as we are sitting here doing nothing.**
- **She looks like she would enjoy a soothing neck massage.**
- **I will kiss her back as we lay and let her how great she is.**
- **I will hold her hand and tell her how much I love her.**
- **Let me go ahead and wash up those dishes so she can relax.**

These are beautiful and loving little things that you can do. They do not cost you any money whatsoever to make them happen. These things could bring her great joy and deep satisfaction. And, you will start to find little pleasures in pleasing her in such a simple and easy ways.

Sadly, because a woman occasionally seeks this kind of physical closeness from you, it causes many men to throw a fit, gripe, moan and cry like a baby! His story is that he is tired or does not feel like doing anything!

The reality of the matter is that a man acting like this is being SELFISH! Your woman wants to be close to you, so shut your mouth. Stop your whining and treat her like a Princess. Every Day!

Think about it for a minute! You want her to give you sexual satisfaction at a moment's notice and be your fantasy dancing queen, ensuring that you are never in need in the sexual realm of your relationship; yet, when she wants some cuddle time, you act as if she has the plague! Not cool at all!

If you are ready to be a "Real Man" you have got to understand this part of man-woman relationships perfectly."

You may be similar to me to where no one ever taught you about the dynamics and inter-workings of a man-woman relationship.

Hey, I get it, because there was time in my past that I had no clue about such things!

But, to change, it only took me one study-book on the subject matter, and my eyes were opened wide from that point forward. Before I had started reading on the topic, I was still and boy in mind, but a man in body.

One of the major objectives of this study-guide book is to assist you out of the darkness and put you in position to do the smart and positives action steps for improving your relationship with your Special Lady.

Some men even add into the mix of the whole ignore and neglect behavior, the stinking attitudes of being mean, grumpy and irritable. In fact, they will even turn around almost every negative situation of events and blame it on his woman.

Look, all your woman wants from you is for you to treat her lovingly and act as though her needs, wants and desires do count and that you are the man to fulfill them.

The reason for this kind of behavior is, again, based on what is rooted in your thoughts. **Your thoughts are selfish and apathetic towards her needs!** For those who want to change this aspect of themselves, there are mental exercises that you can do daily to improve this particular defect, of which you currently display.

As long as you have a burning desire to save your relationship, you should expect positive much-improved actions to arise from within your inner-most being quite naturally.

"Today, I will grab a beautiful bouquet of flowers and surprise her with them."

Let Me Say This Loud and Clear:

Please STOP Demoralizing the Heart, Mind, and Spirit of Your Lady Right Now! STOP Hurting Her "Emotionally!"

Of all the people in her life, you are supposed to be the one that she can come to as a pillar of strength and protection. Instead, you act as if you are her sworn enemy to the death!

You said to her: "do this or do that;" "get this or get that;" and expound profusely on what your "needs" and "desires." The minute she wants a little warm expression of gentleness in the way of hugging, cuddling, snuggling or sitting close to you, however; you damn near have a heart attack!

In fact, some of you act as if, you would rather have a heart attack than provide peace, love, and security in the way of a warm, affectionate embrace with your Precious Lady!

There are many men, now including myself, who find your actions despicable, deplorable and inexcusable. You are destroying a precious and tender hearted-person due to your arrogance, selfishness, lack of insight and lack of compassion for the feelings of the lady who is supposed to be the "Princess of your world."

I would like to strongly recommend that, at this very moment, you do a 180 degree turn around. Be aware of this "highly toxic" and "highly corrosive type of behavior!"

Bro, you are losing her emotionally! She will eventually change and become someone who you no longer know and then, just like that, POOF! She will be gone from your life FOREVER!

I am making a plea to you of epic proportion. Find your lady right now wherever she may be, tell her that you are sorry. Hug her and hold on to her as you have never done before!

From this point forward, crystallize this action into your daily routine of living. You will see and hear how incredibly magnificent it makes the "Love of Your Life" feel.

"I cherish my Precious Lady, and I let her know that by sending a text today."

In case no one has told you, I am saying to you in a rather gentle way that you must realize that you have been very selfish and unkind to your Precious Lady.

Fix This Problem Now

1. Start IMMEDIATELY with the Self-Talk scripts in this study guide.
2. Thoroughly Review **Chapter 12** on Healing Your Relationship.
3. Spontaneously seek her out to hold her hand or hug her, kiss her!
4. Think outside the box, do small little touches and actions of affection!
5. No yelling, swearing or acting like a tyrant who rules with an iron fist!
6. If your time is monopolized by your cell phone and TV sports, Kill them!
7. Dedicate time to focusing on your beautiful lady and doing things with her.

My Personal Plea to You:

I can understand where you are right now because I was there years ago. I needed to fix some things on myself, but I was unsure of how.

You need to know that I was the most supreme a**hole on the planet earth when it came to many of these negative thoughts, horrific bitter speech, and neglectful, selfish actions.

However, I turned it around by a steady input of positive, uplifting information that not only healed me, but the world around me became intensely enriched with goodness and kindness. I was on my way to Becoming a New Man!

You CAN Do This! Your Special Lady is your shining light of love and beauty for you. Don't blow it. Get your act together!

"Yes, I am the Master of my thoughts – I CHOOSE to think good thoughts!"

| I Outwardly Show and Express My Love |

New Man Mind Trainer # 7

I am the kind of man who outwardly and directly shows and expresses my love for my Special Lady in many ways. I seek to invent new ways to let her know how much my heart is devoted to her and her happiness.

I am so happy and pleased that _____, is at my side. I spontaneously hold her and kiss her lips and face. I greet her with hugs and kisses, when I come home from anywhere. I tell her every day that I Love Her.

I will let her know that I adore her, that I cherish her, that she means the world to me. I will unexpectedly hold her close and whisper "I love you" into her ear. I am presenting a "New Me" to her every day. A better me!

Every morning, I smile at her and before we separate and go our own ways in the day, I let her know that I look forward to seeing her soon. *(end of affirmation)*

Must Always Be Done with Intense Desire, Emotion, and Repetition.

| I am No Longer a Man of My Old Ways |

New Man Mind Trainer # 8

I am no longer the man of my old ways, but I am Transformed, and I AM a New Man. My thoughts are New, Fresh, and Gentle in all of life's circumstances and challenges of my day. I say the words, "I am sorry" quickly. I am always humble when doing so.

I am at peace in ALL of my daily work, play and business endeavors. When I am connecting to my Special Lady, she hears the voice of a New Man who is calm and easy-flowing with positive tender-hearted words that are spoken to her.

The power of my new thoughts produces fantastic, new actions that are good, healthy and encouraging that builds the strength of our love and our relationship. I work diligently to continue in my self-improvement journey and I love the awesome growth that I am experiencing EVERY DAY.

Truly, I AM A NEW MAN! I think as a New Man! I speak as a New Man! I act as a New Man! ALL that I do works to heal and shine a beautiful light of a great love and devotion that I have for my Lovely Lady. I AM a New Man! *(end of affirmation)*

"I am always thoughtful, insightful and generous towards the Love of My Life."

CHAPTER 10

Beer, The Boys & Leaving Her Home Alone… AGAIN!

You have chosen your loser friends, beer, partying and drinking yourself into a drunken stupor over the undying and everlasting love of your beautiful lady! **Are You So Foolish?** Where in the hell are the higher functioning intellectual capacities of your brain?

You are a "party animal." You still go out to the clubs and watch the partially naked women dance on stage, with enticing moves of sexuality and lust! <u>However, you temporarily forget all about the ONLY woman that you should be focused on, which is at home waiting for you!</u>

You Are Destroying Her! **She is bleeding profusely deep within her soul, and calling out your name, begging you to stop her pain!**

What gives you the right to be so indignant and completely thoughtless, as to carry on with such reckless abandonment?

Of course, due to your extreme level of selfishness, and the incredibly vast amount of neglect that you have used like a club, to beat her down, you have failed to even consider the fact that you are the central source of her being, so miserable and even depressed!

She is the Problem in Your Mind!

Wake up bro, and smell the coffee!!

The problem is not your lady if you are out doing these kinds of things and leaving her at home alone, as you seek out places to chum around with your buds!

Give Me a Freakin' Break!

"I express my love and appreciation for my Lovely Lady OPENLY every day."

Then, you have the presence of mind to come home and wake her up for a round of wonderful lovemaking with you! HA! You stink with the smell of beer and sweat, yet YOU expect her to perform for you! Worst yet, is that YOU get pissed off when she turns away from your aggressive advances. You go to smother her with your ultra-smooth actions of how to turn a woman on and for some reason they are not working on her. Hmmm! *I wonder why?*

Such actions are TOTALLY laughable! IF this is your mode of operation within your relationship, do you think this is a turn-on for her? Really?

Yes, you will find me absolutely brutally hard on ANY MAN that carries on with this kind of behavior. There's no excuse for it, and a real man should know better!

In fact, any man of average intelligence should know that "it grosses out virtually every woman on earth." It never has any place in a relationship with a lady that you have selected as the "Love of Your Life" or your "Special Love!"

> **O.M.G. URGENT NEWS UPDATE**
>
> What you find cool and sexy (yourself) she finds completely disgusting and 100% repulsive, because you stink and your breath reeks of rancid, burpy, beer breath! For real, bro!

When she goes to complain about your behavior, you line up the firing of swift tactical mind-bending cuss words and a continuous flow of emotionally traumatizing insults. These eventually cause her tears. You leave her to spend another sleepless night contemplating why you act like such a jerk!

If you don't change your ways, one day she will be gone!

Either on her own or with one of your very best friends, who has observed your neglectful and selfish ways, she gets the courage to leave you for someone who she believes will treat her far better. Ain't no joke my friend, it happens every day!

"God has opened my eyes and is leading me to massive personal growth."

Okay, let's be very real about this. In your way of thinking, you believe that it is okay for you to treat her in such a way to where she is ignored, while you deal with your partying, bar hopping and late-night antics!

Perhaps you are one of those guys who are into drugs or other illegal activities. Your lady has asked you to stop, but you have AGAIN ignored her wishes and neglected her feelings about ALL that has taken place over the course of your rotten to the core relationship!

Here is the deal: Women elect to stay with us men who are losers a lot longer than they should! Why? This is because they still love us and are Praying to God Almighty that a miracle occurs, and we GROW UP!

Even when they have clear and ample evidence that we are pathetic in virtually all aspects of communication, faithfulness, and commitment to do the right thing!

AGAIN… you know that I am right about these things. You feel the pressure mounting upon you as you read this information!

This only happens with men who read this kind of detailed relationship information. In their heart, they realize that they are heading down the wrong road with how poorly they have been treating the most important person in their life.

For those of you who do not feel guilty, I feel sorry for you. Your life will be filled with misery and plenty of heartaches that follow you no matter what relationship you are involved with!

I was where you are at one time. I have somewhat of an idea of what is inside of you that causes you to hold firm to rigid thinking that gives you the false belief that you can treat your lady with such low regard and heartless behaviors.

Treating a woman with such low regard is based on thoughts rooted in the kind of information that you have been exposed to regarding women. This kind of hard and crude way of being towards someone who we love is a direct indicator that we developed Dominant Mental Operating Programs of this nature.

"I express my love and appreciation for my Lovely Lady OPENLY every day."

The bottom-line on all of this is that I am not making excuses for our behavior, I am just revealing to you, how most likely, the negative or positive thought process develops in us humans.

All of us, men and women, are all shaped by our previous experiences and information provided to us by family, friends, TV, movies, radio and past relationships. In truth, we have plenty of junk information locked into our brains that screw us up!

The junk information locked in our minds reflects the corrupt, selfish and evil thoughts of our mind, and behaviors that show outwardly how screwed up we are! You may not like reading that, but it is the bold truth.

Though the above two paragraphs may not sound rosy, just know that you CAN turn around your circumstances and move mentally in a much healthier direction. You CAN correct these negative attributes and rewire your brain, thus changing your thoughts, your speech, and your behavior.

Your Special Lady means the world to you! So, by deciding to embrace the power of choice, you can now choose a new path that can be an enriching and beautiful life-changing impact for the both of you, which eventually should lead to a much better relationship.

You have the power to "CHOOSE" the kind of thoughts you want in circulation in your brain. By making this change, you no longer will be the major force that causes her to feel so sad about all of your ridiculously painful actions.

What I have been saying since you started this study-guide book is that you can actually do something about the quality of your thoughts and your actions. Up to this point, you have done NOTHING to help her heal and repair the damage in which you have inflicted on your "Special Lady."

The crazy thing is that you know the EXACTLY WHY she is so sad, emotionally removed and depressed; but up to this point, you have done nothing to help improve the situation, and take away her immense, intense pain and suffering!

"If I am ever angered, I quickly defuse the emotion and gently speak to my lady."

Men, IF you care anything about your lady, then it is time to step up, and begin the process of loving her and treating her the right way! No more excuses or delays!!!

| As I Start Each day I Set My Mind and Mood | New Man Mind Trainer # 9 |

As I start each day I set my mind and mood to being upbeat, optimistic and positive. I truly do love_____, and I show her how much she means to me by my words, my actions and my deeds. I hold her close to begin and end my day and whisper into her ear words of healing and praise.

_____, now hears and sees a New Man because I am a New Man and I present to her a man that has left behind my old ways, but I come to her with the greatness that God has placed inside of me and my new ways.

I am poised, patient and under control of my emotions and NEVER speak harshly to my most precious gift from heaven. I make excellent choices in how I think, and I am thoughtful about _____, needs, wants and special desires. I spontaneously hold her and kiss her lips and face. I greet her with hugs and kisses, whenever I come home from anywhere.

My mood is based upon my thoughts and my thoughts are positive, warm and uplifting because I am a NEW and Better Man!   *(end of affirmation)*

"I am no longer a slave to anger and bad moods - I NEVER speak rudely."

CHAPTER 11

Bad Attitude Dude!

"BAD ATTITUDE? FLUSH IT & MOVE ON!"

ATTITUDE IS A DECISION

moody, angry, grumpy men

Can You Handle the Truth?

We Choose Our Attitude! Good or bad attitude, it is ALWAYS a deliberate thought to be nice or not nice!

Wait a freakin' minute! You mean to tell me that you came home from work and acted like a terrorist the moment you walked through the door to greet your Special Lady? Hold on! What do you think you are doing? Why are you doing this?

What excuse do you dare present that allowed for such behavior? Buddy, I have some news for you! There is not a single excuse in the world that you can tell me that should cause you to walk through the door, day after day, and treat her with such a mean and callous attitude!

Coming home from work, play, or wherever; you should come home to your Precious Love with the mindset that you are going to express your immense joy for her. You should ONLY come toward her with healthy, positive energy because you are finally back at home. You can gaze your eyes upon that Lovely Special Lady in your life. Upon seeing her, you should always be "excited," and your eyes should sparkle because she is now in your sight! *(You deliberately choose to be one way or the other.)*

Sadly, all across the world, many men will come home from work, play, the bar or whatever and they will treat their ladies like total crap! They are whining, groaning and moaning about ridiculous, pitiful and immaterial subject matters. Often times, they are taking out their irritability and stinking attitude on their lady!

Your woman does not know if she should speak to you or not. She doesn't know what she needs to do, so that you do not take it out on her with your cursing, yelling and highly irritable attitude.

"I NEVER speak sharply, rudely or harshly, to my Precious Lovely Lady."

So, in your mind, you think that it is okay to be this way, or that it is normal for the kind of situation that you are in? She should not take it so seriously.

What has gone wrong with you to where you can treat her with such intense fiery scorching anger that burns long and hot?

First of all, that kind of temperament is not emotionally healthy or kind anywhere in the world! <u>You deliberately act this way because you have done it for many years. Secondly, you have elected to think negative thoughts and then vomit ruthless irritable speech and actions towards your Special Lady who loves you so much.</u>

In a very nice way of telling you this; You ARE Wrong!

Some people (men in this case) just wake up in the morning being pissed-off about who knows what, but they are irritable and cranky, and they let you know it. I have known so many men who are like this, and I also used to be like that too!

Once I started going through my transformative learning process to be a New Man, I concluded a few things that are now proven science.

We <u>Deliberately</u> Choose to Act on Our Thoughts!

If you have negative traits and attitudes about yourself that are poor for healthy communication and bad for relationships, <u>you CAN change them</u>!

You Just Need to Have the COURAGE to Do So!

The reason why these negative aspects of our personality exist is that we developed them over the years. It has become our way to handle the circumstances of life.

Typically, it is a combination of our interaction with people who were **Highly Sensitive Role Models,** and many directly related or similar life experiences that developed this kind of mindset within us.

<u>Our brain is a massive recording and storage device.</u> It will cause you to think and act in the direction of your most Dominant Mental Operating Programs that you have developed from life experiences.

A Dominant Mental Operating Program or mental operating script is usually formed in us because of repeated exposure to a particular stimulus. One other way to acquire a dominant program is from shocking one-time-events.

"In the morning, I greet my love with a smile and joy."

The truth of the matter is that you are now taking her for granted. You are partying, drinking and leaving her at home by herself on many nights without a thought of consideration for how this may be causing her to feel.

She is nothing more than an occasional sex toy to you! When she attempts to speak about her feelings and where the relationship is heading, you blow her off and tell her that she is exaggerating or that she is a "pain in the butt!"

This woman has loved you, even with all of your faults. Your insincere "cold as ice" behaviors flow undeservedly to her, and you rarely confess words of love to her!

Waking up in the morning, you rarely ever speak to her with more than a grunt or two! In fact, you complain about the fact that she is bugging you when she asks any kind of questions about your day or the upcoming weekend activity schedule!

Why so mean? Why so grumpy? Why such irritability and a rotten attitude?

Here are 3 Important Questions for You to Answer:

- **Why so damn grumpy and so hateful towards the "Love of Your Life?"**
- **Why do you continue to inflict such cruel and undeserving pain into her precious heart, and gentle flowing spirit?**
- **What is your freakin' problem, to where you are so blind to the pain that you are causing her?**

Here is a shocker! No matter what answer you gave, you are wrong! IF YOU THINK that any woman you claim to love or care about deserves that kind of treatment, **You Are Dead Wrong!**

STOP MAKING ALL THOSE LAME AND WORTHLESS EXCUSES!

Consider this: she cries many times in her day without you even being aware of it! She is so careful not to cause you to get pissed-off. She hides many of the days when she has been miserable, depressed and crying rivers of tears in solitude!

Moreover, you are so selfish and only think of yourself. You failed to see all the emotional trauma, scarring, and pain that you inflicted upon her almost every single day of her life! Does such hateful, hurtful and abusive language make you feel like more of a man? If so, you need to examine the content of your heart closely!

"I am no longer a slave to anger and irritability - I ALWAYS speak and act gently."

A "Real Man," ALWAYS treats his lady with the utmost respect in ALL circumstances, because he is thoughtful, and in control of his thoughts, actions and behaviors!

Moody, Angry & Grumpy Men here is how you are affecting the most special and precious person in your life:

- She secretly cries, and she is depressed!
- She feels insecure and useless!
- She is afraid of making a mistake!
- She is nervous and cannot sleep!
- She looks run down and tired!
- She avoids you most of the time!
- She stays over at friends place often!
- She is beginning to resent you!
- She uses alcohol or drugs to escape!
- She may even contemplate suicide!

I hope that there is a voice inside of you that says treating her like dog excrement is dead wrong, and you want to stop, NOW!

Think about it!

You claim that you love her, <u>yet nearly all of your actions</u> have been showing the complete the opposite! Your behavior shows that you do not understand the meaning of love or that you feel she is not worthy of love. ***It is time to change all of that!***

Yes, You Are Destroying Her Emotionally!

Do you mean to tell me that you are so miserable that you cannot control your basic emotions, nor are you able to treat her with kindness upon waking up in the morning?

You do not qualify to call yourself a "**Real Man!**" A "**Real Man**" is in complete control of such barbaric, primal-Neanderthal-like behaviors and actions that can destroy a woman!!!

"This learning comes easy to me - I am excited about my New Man's Mind Journey."

Once you decide to be a "**Real Man**," you suddenly realize the crudeness of your stupid grunts that you provide as sentences, are entirely un-interpretable!

A "Real Man," ALWAYS treats his lady with the utmost respect in ALL circumstances, because he is thoughtful, and in control of his thoughts, actions and behaviors!

He does not blame his grumpiness on the morning, or the weather, a bad day or watching the game. He is not grouchy upon just waking up from a nap, or on 49 other made-up reasons!

He DOES NOT offer excuses for treating the "Love of His Life" like garbage! He DOES NOT swear at her or tear her down! **He only seeks to build her up as the crowning jewel of his life!**

In fact, a "Real Man" lifts his Princess up whether he is near or far. He is considerate and kind, regardless of the other distractions and concerns in life. She and her feelings are more important to him than anything else!

If you find that you cannot or will not do this for the lady in your present relationship, then please let her go!

Come on, bro! Free her from your evil and almost demonic like behavior!! You have to know already that you are insensitive, thoughtless and selfish, whenever you carry out the numerous verbal abuses and scathing verbal attacks on your precious lady.

Since you are relatively sure that this kind of behavior is not emotionally healthy for her, then STOP right now with the horrific and destructive verbal barrages!

We are speaking about her and how your tirades of ugly verbal smack-downs affect her. What most never figure out is that these kinds actions also further corrupt you psychologically as a man, each time you do it. <u>It makes it much more difficult for you to stop. You would most likely, STILL be acting out this way, even if you were in a new relationship. This is a hardened Dominant Mental Operating Program for you.</u>

Vulgar, Demeaning and Bullying Language

So, you are a "**Bad Attitude Dude.**" Your lady calls you out on this, and your response has been to launch into a high-powered verbal assault of foul-mouth-beat down language that incinerates the flesh off of her bones and rips at the very fabric of her tender soul!

"I am no longer a slave to anger and irritability - I ALWAYS speak and act gently."

You look to teach her that you are the boss, and you hurl an incalculable amount of mind-numbing "F-bombs" at her so that you can crush her mentally and emotionally!

At point-blank range, you surgically fire out a series of scornful and cruel remarks that are designed to make her succumb to your might and power. *Oh boy, such a man!* For real, my friend, doesn't this feel WRONG? I hope so!

Based on those kinds of actions, it seems that you take such joy in ripping to shreds the heart and emotional faculties of your "Special and Most Precious Lady."

Let me be sure I understand, you are pissed-off because she pointed out to you that you are grumpy, moody or have a bad attitude. Then, you proceed to curse and swear at her non-stop until her tears are gushing forth like a fountain!

Some of you have verbally and emotionally traumatized your Lovely Lady so much that she has no more tears to cry for you! This is a major red flag that you are nearing the point of losing her permanently!

Oh yeah, you think that this now makes you the big man of her life?

You are so wrong! In truth, these kinds of actions just make you tiny and insignificant! Your tongue only weighs a mere 4 ounces, and yet, you do not have the power to control it, nor what is blurted forth from your foul mouth!

Your tongue has the power to build up, or to tear down!

Your spoken words have the power to give life to the heart, mind, and spirit. They can also steal and suck the life out of the emotional fabric of your Princess!

Your Vile and Wicked Mouth is a Cesspool of Toxic Poisonous Waste! It readily spews forth flaming, incendiary verbal beat-downs, into the heart and soul of the "Lady of Your Life" and it will eventually, completely destroy her emotionally and your relationship with her!

What will it be? From this point forward, you can make a positive difference and change for the "Love of Your Life!" However, you must invoke the power of "CHOICE," to make the best decision in this matter!

For those of you who what to change, and make a bright, fresh new start — you must understand that the actions required for making the change MUST repeatedly be applied with a burning desire to change!

"I treat my Precious Lovely Lady with the highest level of respect at ALL times."

It starts by being aware of your extremely negative and evil-guided attitude and actions towards your "Lovely Lady!" It is **YOUR MIND,** and it is **YOUR MOUTH**. <u>**You Control Them Both!**</u> So, "Man-Up" and use the power of "CHOICE" to make better decisions **STARTING NOW!**

She is waiting for you right now to confess that your behavior has been terrible towards her! So, get busy, go to her and hug her! Hold her firmly and tell her that you love her and apologize for how you have been, and how poorly you have treated her!

This begins the healing process and starts to free the both of you from the shackles and chains of miserable and hurtful communications.

Something about him scares me... Will he be violent next time?

"I instantly correct negative thoughts and immediately outwardly speak positively."

Your Anger Has Given Birth! There is a huge problem with being in a "Ready-to-Go-Angry" state of existence that is rarely discussed, and this that it gives birth to other negative attributes of personality.

The three Primary Ones Are combativeness, resistant and ignorance. However, let me first clear up what I mean here. **All of us get angry.** It happens to all of us at some time or another. In fact, anger at times can be a good thing — if it is well-managed.

Mind you, the kind of anger that causes enormous problems is usually characterized by the following "*flash anger*", "*hair-trigger irritability*" or anger that is "*ready-to-go-anger.*" **These hyper states of anger or irritability are UGLY!** There is NOTHING good about them, and they are NEVER well-managed! The truth is, you are just pissed off, and you want to just roll with it.

My own anger consisted of the above descriptions. **My kind of anger was UGLY, and I was ignorant to the fact that it was a problem!** I thought it was someone else's fault for MAKING ME angry. I could not see that I was WAY WRONG, because of my Dominant Mental Operating Programs that were well-developed within me in the early years of life.

I will also admit to you that the vast majority of my thinking (until I was about 28 years old) was negative, defective and corrupted. My whole world view was formerly based on all those toxic, ugly thoughts and a poor self-image. In other words, the views I had in life on how I was supposed to think, and act were severely jacked-up!

This kind of attitude that I had with this ready-to-go-anger and hostility was brought on by just being irritable from almost anything. Living this way SUCKS!

Sadly enough, MANY men live with this kind of razor-sharp edge. Then, once they speak to their special someone, they direct this senseless verbal cesspool of rotten trash at the innocent person, whom they supposedly love and care about.

Stop trying to rationalize and justify the ridiculous defense that you have the right to be angry. Of course, you have the right to be angry, but let's keep in mind that I am discussing the management of your anger, and to whom you are directing it. Good grief, man! Wake Up!

"I am always seeking the kindest words and actions that lift my woman's heart."

Your woman is in mental turmoil because of your mismanaged bouts of anger. She has to catch the heat and negative energy of your "bad days." Though you were pissed off with your co-workers, crazy drivers on the road, money lost with sports gambling, and numerous other things that make you angry, she is the one who catches your bitter-stinking-thinking words and actions.

It is important to remember that if we hold onto a particular negative personality trait, especially those that govern the quality of interpersonal relationships, we most likely are damaged with a host of other characteristics that are also barriers to a loving, sensitive heart and excellent communication.

If you live in this state of being angry, or rapidly shift there, here are three other negative traits to which you also have given birth. These make it extremely difficult for your Special Lady to communicate with you effectively.

3 Ugly Offspring of Your Anger

Combativeness – *def.* to fight against. This seems to be almost by nature, by which this kind of person does this. They seem to reject new information or correction or assistance for self-improving. Many times, mentioning anything related to your anger only seems to irritate you. The position that you tend to take is to be more of an adversary and looking to create negative energy.

Resistance – *def.* to block or to oppose. Yes, it makes sense that with the anger problem, a person would put up barriers and many times be very closed-minded. You refuse to listen or learn. You only become angrier!

You reject honest conversation, and are prone to rapid anger and walking away from your Lovely Lady when she attempts to make healthy communication with you.

Ignorance – *def.* to have lack of knowledge. And sadly, you make decisions without having knowledge or information that is adequate. You just shut-down further conversations and will not take the time to shut-up and listen to the complete message. Ignorance about yourself and how to communicate is a death sentence to the relationship.

Nearly everything you argue about with your Special Lady with has to do with how you "feel," instead of what is fair and right. Seriously, you "feel" justified with your bouts of mismanaged anger and rage.

"I show the lighter side of life in situations that are challenging."

If you are one of these angry, grumpy and moody kind of men, it goes without saying that there is a 98% chance that you are combative, resistant and ignorant.

The words that I write to you are straight-forward and blunt. So, let me say upfront that none of this that I write to you is a put-down. I am just giving you real talk! And yes, I want you to know that I was practically the same way with my negative characteristics of my personality.

With that being said, I am letting you know right now, **You CAN fix this junk!**

IF you have the desire to change and self-improve, then it WILL happen!

Your grumpy, moody and highly irritable ways most likely are defective programs that were created by you many years ago. This is just the way you have always being. Now that you are Consciously Aware that you may have a problem, I want you to live every day with the highest of confidence, that you CAN correct it.

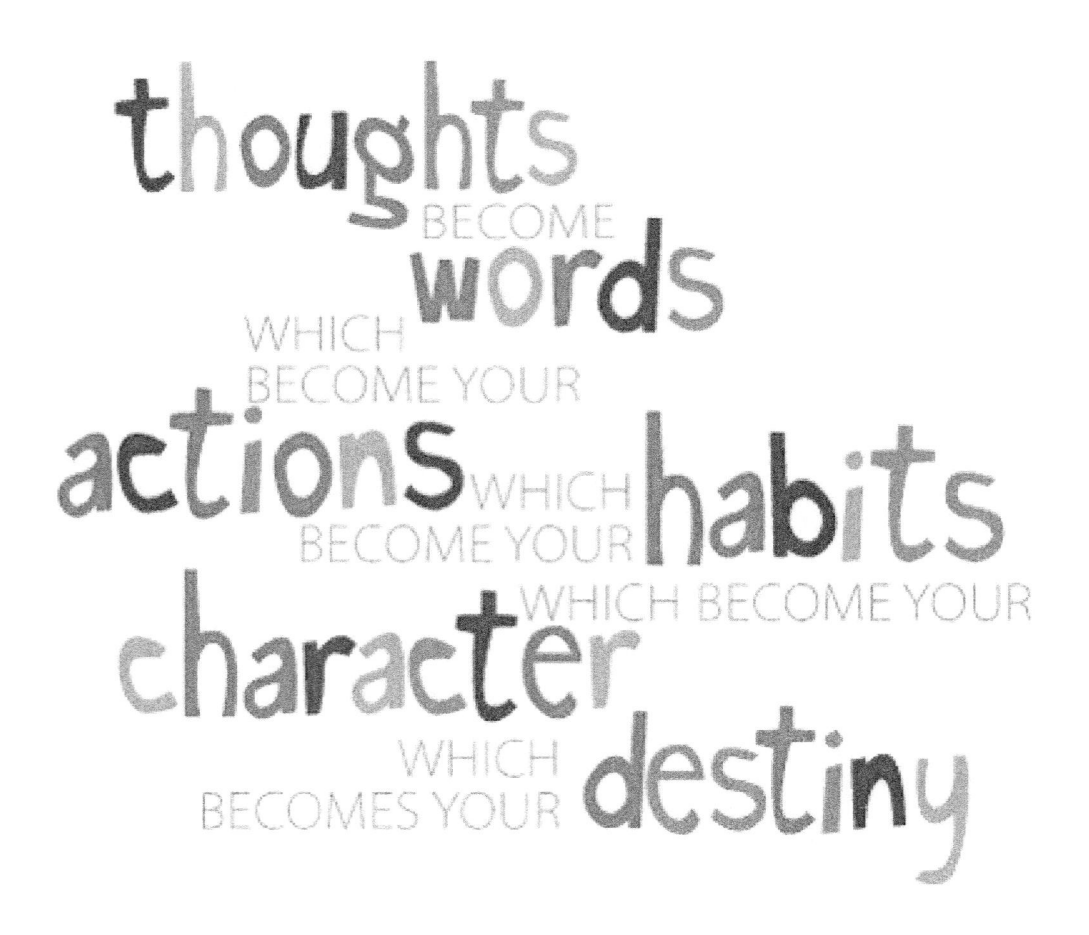

thoughts BECOME *words* WHICH BECOME YOUR *actions* WHICH BECOME YOUR *habits* WHICH BECOME YOUR *character* WHICH BECOMES YOUR *destiny*

"I am optimistic, and I uplift the heart and soul of my Lovely Lady."

No More a Slave to Your Thoughts
but Now You Can Become the Master of Them and Be Transformed into a New Man

For too long, your thoughts have taken you over with negative and destructive words and actions against the most Special Lady of Your Life. In essence, you have been a slave to these thoughts and impulses arising from deep within.

The first step in becoming a better man is to accept the fact that you are the only one that is TOTALLY responsible for your thoughts, your speech, and your actions.

You can ONLY point the finger of blame at yourself for all of your outburst of anger and evil-minded energy created by you, and directed towards your woman or anyone else.

You have been a slave to all of those feelings and emotions that cause you to yell, scream, threaten, demean, degrade, criticize and intimidate. If you are grumpy, moody or irritable: wake up. You have been a slave to those negative attitudes.

You now have the opportunity to become the Master. The Master is ALWAYS aware of his thoughts, and work towards improving the quality of his thoughts. The Master directs his tongue in a positive and uplifting manner; providing words of encouragement, praise, and love. The Master strives for the goal of steadily self-improving and becoming a better person for his friends, family and for sure his Special Lady in life.

So, make the choice. Do you want to become the Master?

Or, do you just prefer to continue being a slave?

Consider your answer carefully because one takes work and the other does not.

"I am consciously aware of my thoughts, and I flow with positive actions."

Brain Training Instructions

This simple routine will begin the process of building new Neural-Networks for you that gradually improves your thoughts and actions.

Desire, Emotion, and Repetition are Paramount to Your Success.

- <u>Read it to yourself 10-12 times per day for the next two days.</u>
- <u>On the third day, speak it outwardly multiple times throughout the day</u>.
- Always Perform with Focus - No Distractions!
- Turn OFF the radio and put that damn cell phone down!
- Read two times as you awaken BEFORE you get out of bed!
- Read two times during your morning coffee and/or morning work breaks.
- During the day make a quick phone call; tell your lady kind and loving.
- Send her one text to communicate words of endearment to her.
- Read two times BEFORE you walk in the door to greet your woman.
- Greet your lady with a warm, tender embrace when coming through the door.
- NEVER walk through the door on your cell phone. All attention directed to her.
- Read two times before you go to bed and contemplate the words spoken.
- Always read with intense feelings of emotion. Make yourself feel it deep!

Train your mind in the direction that you want it to go!

No longer accept negative, corrupt and useless program scripts that only serve to pollute your mind, poison your thoughts and harden your heart.

How long have you been Unconsciously Unaware of what the sources of programming your brain was and how they have shaped your thinking?

Hopefully, by now, your eyes are beginning to open. You can go forth to Awaken the Sleeping Giant of Greatness in you!

No longer are you a victim who has been held hostage with self-imposed mental chains of bondage, unproductive wayward thoughts, and actions. **Since you have made the decision to grow, you are now the Victor!**

As the victor, you can change the world around you and improve the relationship with your precious, Lovely Lady and all others in your life.

"I am growing in my efforts to self-improve every day."

> **I am a New Man and as a New Man**
>
> **New Man Mind Trainer # 10**
>
> I am a New Man and as a New Man, I now create new thoughts that are fun, bright and cheerful. I know that I am the sole controller of my own thoughts and from this day forward, I dwell on what are good and uplifting thoughts that I will boldly speak to my lovely lady EVERY DAY! Right now, I am thinking how I can be better. I am Consciously Aware of my thoughts, my spoken words and my physical actions and I only bring forth that which is beautiful, gentle, kind and loving. I ONLY speak to _____, with words that insightful, encouraging, peaceful, uplifting and loaded up with an abundance of love. I am a New Man. I am her New Man. A better man who is transforming to become the very best that I can in treating _____ in the most beautiful of ways! *(end of affirmation)*

Yes, your own words read and spoken out loud to yourself have the power to rewire your brain and give rise to new, good, positive and healthy relationship thoughts. (*Desire, Emotion, and Repetition are the key*)

> **The is a New Day! It is a New Beginning**
>
> **New Man Mind Trainer # 11**
>
> This is a New Day! It is a new beginning to where I am embracing the joy of being alive. I am refreshed, and I am energetic to succeed in all things that I do on this day! My attitude is positive, and I have strong Positive Expectancy in the actions of the day. I greet my family and my friends with warmth, optimism and kindness. When something disturbs my attitude, I read and speak positive affirmations. When negative circumstances arise, I am relaxed and at ease because I know that I will find a positive solution. I am designed for greatness. This is a New Day and I WILL Make It a Great Day! Starting Now! So, I go forward and kiss, hug and praise the lady of my life. *(end of affirmation)*

"I am at peace and calm in all of the activities of my day."

CHAPTER 12

Men, Let the Healing Begin!

Learning How to Say, "*I am Sorry!*"

This is the most powerful tool in your "love treasure chest" of items that you have. But you must know how to use these 3 little words!

When an apology is necessary, most who made the offense will say, "I apologize." So, I ask you, "What is that all about?" Are they talking to a business associate or someone who they barely know? Also, and even worst, I will hear people <u>mutter</u> the words, "Sorry." What exactly is that supposed to mean???

Let me get this straight. You actually say "sorry" to someone who you have just hurt or offended. You think that is supposed to help the matter and build a sturdy bridge that unifies your hearts??

Well, just to give you a little keen insight into this matter, the next time you make a grave mistake or has done something that may have hurt your partner, try the full phrase or sentence of **"I am sorry," or "I am very sorry."**

If you really need to go the distance because you blew it, try **"I am so sorry, and it will not happen again."** These words work wonders, and IMMEDIATELY begins the healing of one's heart!

For most of us men, this is our "Achilles Heel" in our relationship!

<u>When we make a mistake, we should immediately own up to it, and then, speak the words "I am sorry" humbly and sincerely.</u>

This is a personal growth opportunity where you should recognize that our egos have no place in re-building or repairing a broken relationship! Saying the words "I am Sorry" or "I'm Sorry" can be part of the cleansing process. If done with the full sincerity of heart, it can be a way of healing for both of you.

"I say the words 'I'm Sorry' with ease, sincerity and lots of love."

This is not a matter of being weak because you do it. It shows that you are strong and that you are becoming more in-tune with kind of actions that are necessary to heal a broken relationship and to begin the process of mending the heart of your Precious Lady.

We, as men, MUST take the lead role in this healthy restoration process! The healing and repair are within our abilities. However, first on the list is that w**e MUST flush the ego down the toilet** and get "real" with our "Special Lady."

Caution: **Women can easily sense an insincere, low-life rat of an apology. So, you better be sincere in heart, mind, and spirit, when in the act of speaking the words, "I am Sorry."**

Examples of What to Say and How to Apologize

To bolster and strengthen your apology you can add the words:

- I am very sorry. Please forgive my actions.
- I am sorry! I promise this will not happen again!
- Please forgive me for my actions; I am truly sorry.
- I am sorry, baby. I showed poor judgment, and it won't happen again!
- I am so sorry, my love. What do I need to do from here?
- Baby, I was wrong. I am very sorry. Please forgive me.

At first, you may need to practice these kinds of statements because you are not comfortable in speaking this way. Just go to the mirror and practice. Make these words a part of the *New You*!

Need Stronger yet? Try the high-powered apologies on the next page! Note: Throw your "ego" in the garbage! It is time to be a "Real Man" and swallow your pride! Do you want her? Then, get to work with the information directly below.

"I say the words 'I'm Sorry' with ease, sincerity and lots of love."

> **Warning:** If you use any of these heavy-duty apology statements, you better be ready to be that new man going from this point forward. **In Fact, before you use these kinds of apologies, you should already be in the process of becoming a new man!** If you screw up in a major way, after delivering such an apology, kiss your life with this Lovely and most Precious Lady good-bye!

Extreme Apologies Examples

_____, I have been a complete jerk. I now realize that. I would be humble and honored to have your forgiveness. Baby, I am so sorry, and I can promise you, that it will happen again!

_____, Listen to me. I have failed you in so many ways. I have not been the man that you have needed me to be. That is now my commitment to you! I am so sorry, and I am asking you for your most loving forgiveness. Please allow me back into your heart! I will not fail you again!

_____, You are totally right! I am totally and completely wrong! I have made many mistakes, and I have let you down in a monumental way. I need your forgiveness, and I am letting you know that I am truly sorry for my reckless actions and terrible behavior! It is my promise to you and God as my witness; this will NOT ever happen again! Just give me the chance to prove myself to you! Please!

_____, I am asking you to forgive me, I know that I did wrong and my promise to you is that it will never happen again. I am currently in the process of change and working towards the kind of man that you need me to be!

Please understand that even when you do these kinds of apologies, it could still take some time for your Precious Lady to get comfortable with the idea that this is really a New Transformed Man standing before her. Be Patient and stay on the path. It is your everyday thoughts and actions that will show her, you are real.

The Basic Rules of the Apology are:

- No ego or pride involved in your delivery.
- Admit guilt and acceptance of responsibility.
- Speak SOFTLY. Be gentle. Be humble. Be sincere.
- Be specific about what you are apologizing.
- Acknowledge that you will guard against making the same error again.

Actions that should help with your cause:

- Down on one knee. (*sometimes humor helps*)
- Holding her hand and stroking it.
- Look directly into her eyes.
- Opening your heart and spilling your guts.
- Quickie love note is given at the time of the apology.

"I say the words 'I'm Sorry' with ease, sincerity and lots of love."

When apologizing for anything the critical thing is to make sure that you are sincere in the apology and sensitive to what you did! This will help from making the same mistake in the future.

Now, just so that we have a fantastic understanding of how to apologize to your special lady here is how you are supposed to NEVER apologize to anyone!

Death Sentence Apology

Never make an apology that is stated, *"I'm sorry, but…"*

I'm sorry, but…

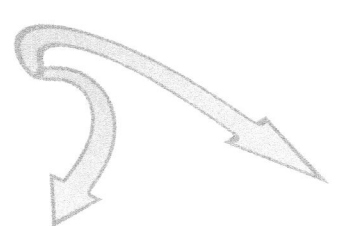

- ✓ You provoked me
- ✓ I was drunk
- ✓ It was actually your fault
- ✓ I didn't mean it
- ✓ I was having a bad day
- ✓ The timing was off
- ✓ I love you
- ✓ I'm an addict
- ✓ I was sleepy
- ✓ I was tired
- ✓ You're wrong
- ✓ You're annoying
- ✓ I was really horny
- ✓ You need some help
- ✓ I just can't help myself
- ✓ I had a bad childhood
- ✓ The stars were crossed
- ✓ Mercury was in retrograde
- ✓ I was really hungry
- ✓ I lost money on the game

<u>You show her that you truly do care and are aware of what you have done when you say the words, "I'm Sorry" with no excuses attached justifying your actions.</u>

<u>NEVER Make the Above Stated Apology Under Any Condition.</u>

"I say the words 'I'm Sorry' never justifying my wrong behavior."

Here are Several Great Add-ons When Saying "I'm Sorry."

I'm So Sorry;

- I feel terrible.
- I really regret it.
- I'm so mad at myself.
- I am so ashamed.
- Forgive me, please.
- I know I hurt you.
- Just a little smile.
- I should have never said that.
- I was TOTALLY wrong.
- You are TOTALLY right.
- It was wrong OF ME to do that.
- I should not have done that.

Pay Attention!

Darn good ways to say the words, **"I'm Sorry"** and a little bit more.

Remember, you show courage and strength as you apologize for mistakes that you make. Your Precious Lady will undoubtedly appreciate your New Attitude & Your Easier Way of Thinking and Being.

"Whenever I must apologize it is always easy for me to do."

Power Moves that Shows You Are Big Time Serious!

You can also bring a gift or set up a special dinner for your apology! Bonus moves that you can make to improve the effectiveness of your apology are to clean yourself up by cutting your hair, shave, trimming your fingernails and toenails, where a pleasant cologne fragrance (maybe her favorite) and be dressed sharp and looking like a million bucks!

The point in all of this is to project a new image for yourself and to let her know that you are not "playing any games" and that you are dead serious about your apology!

"Is this flower big enough to get me out of trouble?"

"This is a new day, and the entire day, I am at peace with all that I do."

CHAPTER 13

Breaking the Cycle of Negative Thoughts and Words.

Your Thoughts Create Your Future — POSITIVE Self Talk

In this chapter, we cover in more detail how you can begin the steady progression of the "New Man Transformative Process." It should be noted that this study-guide book has been structured as it is, to allow for new concepts and ideas to steadily penetrate your mind. This, in turn, activates brain learning neurons and helps in the rewiring of your brain. The process is accelerated with a combination of educational information, affirmations, and New Man Mind Trainer Scripts being presented in a repetitive format. Ultimately, your eagerness to succeed and your desire for personal growth will determine the level of greatness that you will achieve with the program.

At the end of this chapter, there are five powerful New Man Mind Trainer Scripts that you can implement into your Daily Action Plan. You are to make these "Thought Patterns" and "Speech Patterns" a part of you by just reading them and speaking them aloud with emotion 3 to 5 times per day.

The Mental Mind Exercise is known as the process of "**Self-Talk Neuron Activation**." It is what you have been doing as you have been reading the chapters up to this point. IF you have been reading, studying and applying the information, affirmations, and scripts throughout the earlier chapters changes are taking place inside of your brain.

Self-Talk or (internally speaking to yourself) in its most real sense, refers to the organizing of our thought patterns to convince ourselves of something; good or bad. Sadly, most of us have fallen into the trap to use Self-Talk negatively.

Self-Talk is powerful because it does work. In fact, it works exceptionally well, and you have done it thousands of times your entire life. The typical way we use it is to minimize or limit our beliefs regarding our talents, abilities, and gifts.

"It is my mission to be a man showing my Lovely Lady devotion and dedication."

The Self-Image is the Primary Target of Our Self-Talk.

Overwhelmingly and unfortunately, we use the Self-Talk mantra to tear away at our great potential as individuals. We bind ourselves with chains, shackles, and weights around our necks because of the improper use of Self-Talk.

While all of us perform Self-Talk, we may not be fully aware that we are doing it. Though Self-Talk can be done speaking outwardly to yourself, the most common way is with the chatter of your thoughts that you are having in your mind.

Self-talk can be used to build yourself up, or it can tear you down! What is great about Self-Talk is that we can "choose" how we would like to use it; meaning we can use for good or bad!

Here's the real story: All of us of normal mind use Self-Talk every day and have done so for our entire life to convince ourselves that **we cannot** achieve specific goals, talents, skills, dreams, break bad habits or to develop new positive habits. And, above all things, we have <u>unknowingly</u> used it nearly our whole life to destroy our self-image and to think less of our self and abilities.

Research has Shown that 77% of All Self-Talk is Negative! Additionally, keep in mind that 90% of all of our conscious thoughts arise out of the subconscious. WOW! *"Houston, we have a problem!"*

That being the case, I think that we ALL could use some tremendous self-improvement in the area of <u>what we think and why we think, what we think.</u>

To help you along with directing your thoughts and Self-Talk more positively, there are mental exercises termed "**Conscious Compensation Controls.**" They easily guide you to a place of improving your own Self-Talk. As your Self-Talk is influenced by taking advantage of uplifting and encouraging language, new Positive Thoughts will begin to arise and lead your thinking.

The more you repeat the mental and verbal exercises, then more positive thoughts begin to awaken within you.

"I control my thoughts, and my thoughts exudes positive energy."

The Power of Conscious Compensating Controls

> **Conscious Compensating Controls**
>
> Implementing Conscious Compensating Controls involves the willful act of you becoming more Self-Aware that there is a problem and you taking ownership of the problem; Therefore, accepting full responsibility to correct the problem by deliberately invoking emotional conscious effort to displace old, broken, negative and corrupted thinking, speech and behavior patterns.

The repeated action of specific Mental Mind Exercises begins the process of rewiring your brain neurons. You are literally creating a new learning center dedicated to the purpose of being a loving man for your Lovely Lady.

Pay Close Attention: I do not care how long you have been doing things wrong! There is no doubt in my mind that you CAN turn it around! Modern-day brain research science proves that you can override old established patterns and habits as well as learn new ones. This is AWESOME News for all of us. Thank God!

The <u>Mental Mind Exercises</u> work because of how the brain works! Neurons activate and grow connections with other neurons to form highly-energetic, powerful communication centers called "Neural-Networks" that IF directed accordingly can improve thought, speech and behavior. This is how you can correct and improve upon the **old you** and begin development of the **New You**.

<u>These Conscious Compensating Controls will get you there IF you consistently and persistently perform the exercises repeatedly.</u>

At the Speed of Your Thoughts,

You Can Make It Happen!

"At the speed of my thoughts, I eliminate negative thoughts that enter my mind."

Here are your primary set of directives:

Read this to yourself, at least 10 -12 times per day for the next two days. On the third day begin to speak it aloud with intense emotions, UNTIL you feel it is a part of you. Think of what the woman who you love so much mean to you.

- Always Perform with Focus - No Distractions!
- Turn OFF the radio and put that damn cell phone down!
- Read two times before you get out of bed or as you are getting out of bed.
- Read two times during your morning coffee and/or morning work breaks.
- Read two times BEFORE you walk in the door to greet your woman.
- Make a quick phone call and tell her something good, kind and positive.
- Send her one text to communicate words of warmth to her.
- Read two times before you go to bed.
- Always read the with strong feelings and emotion.

Special Note: If you are highly stressed about work or something negative happened in your day. Do some physical activity to release some of that negative energy, so that you don't take it home to greet the lady you love and care so much about such as push-ups, sit-ups, a quick walk around the block.

Cellphone Courtesy: **Do not ever walk into your home to greet the Love of Your Life while STILL on your cell phone.** This boldly communicates that she IS NOT important enough to you for you to greet her with full attention. Make this a hard-fast rule! Your attention needs to be on greeting her with a kiss and a loving smile with your full-undivided attention and focus.

Final Note: You never have to try to memorize it, and over time, you can develop your own, or tweak this one to target any specific improvement that you would like to make for yourself.

"The words that I speak at all times are healthy, good, positive and build-up."

> **I am a New Man - I am Excited**
>
> **New Man Mind Trainer # 12**
>
> **I AM A NEW MAN.** I am excited about my personal growth as I to think and speak in positive terms. I am a new man and I am rapidly improving myself and showing great love and admiration for my lovely lady. I am becoming more of a new man every day because it is good for me and my relationship with the woman who I love. Showing that I have improved is important to me, my friends and my family. I am inspired to become better than I have ever been. I am filled with a heart and spirit of goodness and kindness and it shows itself in the thoughts that I embrace and the words that I speak.
>
> I am a new man and I know that this day will show that truly I am. When I think as a new man my thoughts are about praising my wife/spouse/ girlfriend/fiancé. My thoughts are about the wonderful love that she has shown to me and I need to let her know every day how much she means to me. I am a New Man and I think in terms of finding solutions to problems and being a total help mate to my partner. On this day, I will only think kind thoughts and speak words that lift the heart of the woman who I love so much.
>
> I am a New Man and NOW I will present this New Being to them friends, family and to the world. My journey for self-improving me benefits everyone who I know. In fact, because of my efforts for positive and inspiring thoughts and actions, the world around me is a better place. I am NOW New Man. *(end of affirmation)*

What is happening inside of you is new construction of a neurological and biochemical nature. Your brain in REAL-TIME is actually rewiring HOW and WHAT you think! All you have to do is just keep on doing the mental exercises and affirmations.

Keep on following the process! It is one of those miracles of the creation of your body from God above. The more you do it, the stronger the re-wiring that takes place.

Eventually, New Thoughts will automatically begin to rise to the level of your conscious mind, which over time will replace a lot of those garbage unproductive negative thoughts that used to dominate your thinking.

Get excited my friend, You Are Becoming a New Man; and you are doing it, At the Speed of Your Thoughts!

"At the speed of my thoughts, I instantly correct any of my negative attitudes."

> **The Power of Life and Death is in My Tongue**
>
> **New Man Mind Trainer # 13**
>
> I now know that the power of life and death is in my tongue, so I choose to speak life. I speak words that soothe the heart of my precious lady. I speak words that heals her heart and breathes new life into her soul.
>
> I speak words that are kind, gentle and filled with an abundance of love. I am a New Man and words of life are what I "choose" to speak.
>
> My words flow from my mouth with thoughtful care and a warm tone at ALL times.
>
> There is power in my spoken words, so I am conscientious about the words that I speak to my beautiful lady. My mind produces good and healthy thoughts, so my spoken words are rich, bountiful, and loving.
>
> I cherish and appreciate my sweet lady and my thoughts for her are good, endearing and respectful and the words that I speak to her are precisely the same.
>
> Yes, I am a New Man and EVERY DAY, I speak words that praise her and lifts her heart to the heavens. The power of life and death are in my tongue, I choose words of life that shall be spoken by me to my lovely lady.   *(end of affirmation)*

Must Always Be Done with Intense Desire, Emotion, and Repetition.

> **As a Man Thinks in His Heart So is He**
>
> **New Man Mind Trainer # 14**
>
> As a man thinks in his heart so is he… well then… I AM a NEW MAN! I think with a heart of goodness and kindness to all and I double down on these beautiful actions with my lovely lady.
>
> I think of how I can improve my actions and my spoken words to my lady and what steps I can take to be better as a man. I work enthusiastically to repair and rebuild our love into a love that is fun and filled with awesome beauty, caring and giving.
>
> As a man thinks in his heart so is he… well then… I think of how I can be thoughtful, giving, caring, sensitive, and seek out ways to learn what she needs from me as a man.
>
> I do all of these positive actions, and many more because I am a New Man on a mission to express the depth and breadth of my love for the Love of My Life; not only in words, but also by my actions.
>
> I think like a New Man because indeed I AM A NEW MAN!   *(end of affirmation)*

"Every day I awaken to express my great love for my Precious Lady immediately."

> **I Go Forth into this Day with New Strength**
>
> *New Man Mind Trainer # 15*
>
> I go forth into this day with a new strength and belief in all of the great things that are in me. I have been shaped, fashioned and formed by the hands of God above who placed within me the greatest of talents, gifts and abilities and as a NEW MAN, I live to share only the goodness and greatness of what is in me.
>
> Every Day, I speak with goodness of heart to my precious lady and I bring forth thoughts that express how much she means to me. I bring forth thoughts and actions that show the best of who I am. I show the best of what love can be. The best of what a man of goodness is all about!
>
> My former ways are gone far from me and my new ways spring forth and pour out of me like a fountain from the depths of earth.
>
> Of my great gifts place within me at conception in my mother's womb, I bring them forth to heal the heart of my lovely lady and revitalize our love and build the best relationship possible as this New Man that I am.   *(end of affirmation)*

Must Always Be Done with Intense Desire, Emotion, and Repetition.

> **I Have this Awesome New Day for Me to Begin**
>
> *New Man Mind Trainer # 16*
>
> I have this awesome new day for me to begin, and I shall greet my lady with a huge bounty of gentleness, kindness and love full of passion. My mood, tone and temperament are smooth, easy-flowing and enriching in ALL of my words and actions with my Lovely Lady.
>
> This day is designed to move in the direction of my thoughts, so I am armed with thoughts that are filled with goodness, kindness and patience that are shared among all people who I encounter in my day. But, it starts at home with my beautiful and deserving lady!
>
> _____, is deserving of a man who treat her with pride and joy.
>
> _____, is to have a man who loves her, praises and is kind at ALL times.
>
> _____, is to have a man who only displays positive thoughts and actions at her.
>
> I am that man because I am a NEW MAN filled with thought and actions inspired by my personal growth and self-improvement for being a man who is dedicated and devoted to healing my lady's heart and building a relationship on strength, courage and a vision for treating her as the Princess/Queen of my world. It all begins Today! Right Now!
>
> *(end of affirmation)*

"At the speed of my thoughts, I eliminate negative thoughts that enter my mind."

The Reason this is Necessary? During our lifetime, we have put into our mind a lot of crippling self-image information. For many of us, the thoughts and images that run through our minds are very negative and in some cases evil. In the early stages of life, we had no say in what kind of information went into our mind. Once we are old enough to be on our own, we absorbed information for the most part through Careless Inattention. The combination of early life information and information through Careless Inattention, in part, made us who we are today.

How Do We Change or Improve? The critical mission of this material is to help dilute out the power of the years of that corrupt negative programming, by substituting negative programs with positive and healthy ones. Since 90% of conscious thoughts arise from the subconscious mind, by willfully, enthusiastically, deliberately and repetitively putting new information into your mind eventually, new thoughts will take hold. It is the repetitive action of absorbing new information that creates New Dominant Mental Operating Programs, which can help create a new way of thinking, being and doing. A Transformed Man!

Why Does It Work? It works because that is the science of how the brain works when it comes to learning information. The subconscious mind DOES NOT know if the information is good or bad, positive or negative. Its job is to record and store. Once exposed enough times to a stimulus, it develops the mental response into a Dominant Mental Operating Program and pushes it to the level of our conscious thinking.

You are The Master Programmer. With you becoming Consciously Aware of "what" kind of information is being dumped into your mind. You can now choose only the things that assist you in becoming a better man or better in anything that you have the desire to excel in.

The Bold Truth Is: When fully embracing and living by the information contained within this book, a whole new world of possibilities awaits you!

The science behind why you can be transformed is no mysterious formula, and it is quite simple. Treating your Precious Lovely Lady with the best of heart at all times, under all conditions is a worthy mission. If you have fallen far short or you have personality quirks, attitudes and moods that are damaging to her and the relationship or you are on the brink of losing her, you CAN change. Through repeated application of the Brain-Neuron-Activation Process outline in this powerful life-changing study-guide book for men, you and all who know you will be amazed!

"Once I wake-up to start my day, I give thanks to God for my Beautiful Lady."

Washing Your Brain of the Old While Learning the New

New Information – Nourish your mind with information about the self-image, communication, relationships. This information should be read and even listened to on audio to enhance the effect of having your mind permeated with this New Information.

New Thoughts – New information gives rise to the awakening of the mind, where you begin to generate new thoughts as a direct result of reading and listening to new information. More new information = More new thoughts produced.

New Feelings – Your new feelings naturally arise as new thoughts are streaming vigorously through your mind. Your new feelings challenge your current ones, and some affect your values and how you view the world around.

New Attitudes – Your new feelings eventually cause a change in previously held values and gives birth to new attitudes, which are the foundation for creating a new mindset.

New Beliefs – Your new mindset is the beginning of a person working with new beliefs. These new beliefs come with a whole new way of thinking, speaking, being and doing!

- New Speech
- New Actions
- New Behaviors
- New Habits
- **New Man**

Since you begin to think much differently with the continual input of the new information, this process eventually leads to new beliefs. This means that most likely, you will begin to speak differently also. In addition, your actions, behaviors and habits will make tremendous improvements. This is the process of how we break old bad behaviors and acquire New Healthy ones that fosters the development of a New Transformed Man.

This process works for ANYTHING to where you want to adopt a new skill, talent or ability; whether it is positive or negative. The second critical note here is this is how you became what you are like today, but unfortunately, chances are very high you were not fully aware of the quality of the information entering your mind in those early years of life that were partially responsible for shaping your thoughts.

Here are 3 ways that most of us did receive the information into our brain. The **first way** was through early life growth and development as our parents raised us. The **second way** that we were exposed to high-impacting influences of information into our brain was by done anyone that would be considered a Highly Sensitive Role Model. (HSRM)

"I CHOOSE only thoughts and actions that are positive and build up my Precious Love."

As we get older and start thinking more for ourselves, we put information into our brain by the **third way**, which I describe as Careless Inattention or through being Unconsciously Unaware. No matter which one you want to call it, it means about the same thing, which means, we allow virtually anything and everything into our mind without giving too much thought to how it may be impacting our thoughts and ultimately, our everyday actions.

This is the same exact process of how you learned to ride a bike, type with your thumbs, drive a car, play a video game, play a musical instrument and everything that you have learned with high-efficiency in your life. The crucial fact with this is that you are directing the creation of these new Neural-Networks. You are activating neurons to grow and to form new neural-connections! This means spectacular personal growth is on its way IF you maintain the consistency and persistence of repetitively utilizing the New Man Mind Training Scripts and daily affirmations.

Beginning with this study-guide book and implementing the material in a deliberate, willful, enthusiastic and emotional manner, you start to influence your brain by the **fourth way,** which is done by you being Consciously Aware!

> **From this moment forward, always remember, YOU are now the Master Programmer and Premiere Controller of what goes into your brain! You are no longer a slave to your thoughts, but you are the Master of your thoughts and you CAN custom-tailor design yourself into the kind of man that you want to be. You CHOOSE!**

- Gentlemen, what I have outlined for you in this chapter is how you begin the process of re-wiring your brain and becoming a New and Better Man.

- This is how you will eliminate harmful, useless, corrupted, insensitive and reckless thoughts, speech and behaviors. Desire and Repetition REQUIRED!

- This is how you will create new, permanent, attractive, life-changing positive thoughts, actions, and behaviors that begin healing the heart of the Love of Your Life and save your highly-treasured relationship with your Precious Lady.

- **There are no excuses allowed, my friend. It is time to man-up!**

"At the speed of my thoughts, I instantly correct any of my negative attitudes."

CHAPTER 14

The Most Powerful Language on Earth is Love
Do you know how to speak this language to your special lady?

Love is the most powerful language on earth! Love has healed many who were sick and near death! Love has caused men to be driven and inspired beyond rationale explanations of how!

Love has motivated many humans to work beyond their typical explainable capacities. Love has caused a tidal-waves of change. Many have performed unprecedented feats of physical efforts while under the power of love.

Though I cannot tell you precisely what love is fully; <u>I can tell you that it is not harsh or being mean towards your partner. Love does not scream or shout at one another. Love does not tear down or belittle the person with whom you are in love with!</u>

Love does not swear, curse, or say toxic poisonous words to the one you love! Love does not call the one who you love names such as; stupid, idiot, bastard, bitch, slut, as_hole, son-of-a-b_tch or f_cker. With love there is no name calling. EVER!

You would think that these names were pretty bad, but it can get even worse with words such as c_nt, and motherf_cker. How can you ever claim to love your Precious Lady when yelling, screaming and hurling insulting and entirely demeaning names to her as described above, or worse?

The way I see it, anyone who purchased this book realizes that they have created a regretful situation for themselves and are looking for ways to fix it. Well, this study-guide can put you on the right path to fixing a host of relationship problems.

In the previous chapter, you learned that saying, "I am sorry," is essential in the healing process. Now, we must take your learning to a whole new different level.

"Mastery of Your Tongue," and the words that you allow to flow from your mouth is <u>absolutely vital for you to show or to prove</u> that you are changing and begin the process of earning your Lovely Lady's confidence again!

<u>Remember, you must continue to study more of these kinds of books and materials in order to change what you think and how you think. In turn, they will help you to modify **"how"** and **"what"** you speak!</u>

"My beautiful lady desires lots of love, and I am just the right man for the job."

As a stark reminder, the reason you think the way that you did, and speak the way that you did is because of the Dominant Mental Operating Programs that were embedded in your brain. The way you create new programs that are healthy, clean, positive and uplifting, is by exposing yourself to fresh, high-quality information that reflects what or who you want to become.

So, if I was a complete tyrannical ruling, hardened to the core bully to my Lovely Lady and cursed, screamed and demeaned her that was because my heart was full of hateful and poisonous toxic thoughts. Meaning, those were the Dominant Mental Operating Programs at work within my subconscious mind.

My Freedom Came in the form of "New Information." Once, I started reading a couple of books, listened to audios and speaking some affirmations that I had written, my brain was redesigning itself and began producing New Thoughts that would lead me to new speech and new behaviors. This is the secret to freeing yourself from the old, undesirable and destructive ways of being.

The information that I am arming you with is designed to assist you in having victory over the *old you*! To guide you through the process of making life-changing transformative changes that eliminate broken and destructive patterns that you have utilized to crush the mind heart and spirit of the Love of Your Life.

This is how I learned to give the profoundly enriching and expressive love and affection. This is how I started to think of her in the best of ways! This is how I began to praise her! This is where I learned how to surprise her with little Treasures of My Heart by doing soul-warming acts of kindness and love. This is how I became transformed, enriched and enlightened. This is how you too can if you just have the desire and repeat the actions outlined in this information that CAN set you FREE!

You must begin learning the "Language of Love." The best way to get a handle on this is to "think and be love." So, in every action that you engage in with your Precious Lady, you should **ALWAYS Lead With Love!**

This means that, regardless of the problem or situation, you will ONLY lead with love! In learning how to do this, it will require self-control on an entirely new level for you, because it will require a low-key, non-inflammatory response EVERY TIME!

You MUST BE resolved in your mind and heart that the days of calling her scathing and vile names are unconditionally done!

"I say the words 'I'm Sorry' with ease, sincerity and lots of love."

Remember, it is now your time to shine brightly and be that beam of brilliant, radiant light that warms her soul and shows that indeed a New Man is standing before her!

The beauty and power of this reformation of yourself are that you get to CHOOSE how you want to be! You can charter a healthy, new direction for your relationship. Yes, the power of CHOICE is yours, and can be used to now create a world of profoundly enriching love that is abundant with kindness, and peace!

Let's attempt to find a definition of "Love."

"A deep and tender feeling of affection for or attachment or devotion to a person. An intense feeling of positive emotion toward or the enjoyment of a person, especially strong romantic feelings between two people."

Men, let's get ready for some critical lessons on love and what you need to understand, so that you can begin your growth in this vital area of life.

If you need help or a quick answer for an issue here is my e-mail: Jeff@HowToBeABetterDude.com My answers will be short, to the point and spoken with truth and a caring heart. Just make sure that you give the real story with no junk, or exaggerated information when seeking a solution to your situation.

It is Time to Be a Real Man *(so grow a pair!)*

Principle #1 - Be your own independent thinker and stop listening to most of your friends about how to treat women. Their stupid, ridiculous methods of relationship repair don't matter. Women love a man that can make his own mind about anything, and not need the approval of the boys that you hang out with!

Principle #2 - Start reading books like this, listening to audios and writing affirmations that you speak out every day to increase your learning and rapid ascent into becoming a new man.

Trust me on this, most of your friends will not understand the new man you present to them. Your Special Lady may at first, think that your new attitude is odd. She may not even trust you with it for a while but fear not and hold steady the course!

This is perfectly understandable. Your mission is to be loving, patient and kind, while you keep on improving and remolding yourself as you continue to learn more about love and relationship building.

"As a New Man, I always treat my lady with a tender heart."

Principle #3 - You want to clean up your act! This means that you will dress sharp, be clean and smell fresh most of the time that you are around your lady! This is not the time to be looking like a bum!

This is especially true during the initial phases of rebuilding yourself! Here's why! You are attempting to project a "million-dollar image in attitude." There is no better way to convey this by looking good and sounding good!

Principle #4 - The foul-mouth language and the harsh, abrasive tonality of your statements when you speak must stop! You must remove the negative, condescending words and fiery speech pattern from your mouth!

The Power of Life and Death is in the Tongue

Remember, your tongue only weighs a mere 4 ounces, but it is mighty and can perform astounding wonders to "heal" or to "hurt!" Now, you will strictly use your tongue to heal and no longer will you use it to inflict pain on Your Most Precious Love!

Principle #5 - <u>You are always in complete control of yourself!</u> This means not even a hint of old habits and reactions such as, rolling of the eyeballs, frowning, interrupting, intimidation, fist clenching and fist- pounding. NO MORE! **You will be a Real Man and Lead with Love!**

These changes are not tough, yet they are non-negotiable!

Since your mission is to save your relationship and present a "new image," then you MUST start by becoming **Super Self-Aware** of "what" you are thinking and "how" you are thinking the vast majority of time during your waking hours!

Becoming Self-Aware or Consciously Conscious means that you are sensing your thoughts immediately upon their arrival into your conscious mind. It is at this point to where you can assess if those thoughts are positive or negative. If those thoughts are negative, then you can replace them with positive ones.

This CAN Happen At the Speed of Your Thoughts!

Make no mistake about it, If you master being aware of your thoughts, you will be more conscious of "**what you say**" and "**how you say it.**"

"Becoming a better man means I protect the heart of my Precious Love."

<u>The replacing of old, destructive and corrupt thought patterns with thoughts that are positive, kind, uplifting, humorous or filled with praise and love will cause your speech and physical actions towards your Lovely Lady to be well received.</u>

Think about how you would feel if the Love of Your Life screamed at you, swore at you, belittled you, ignored you, rarely came home, discontinued meaningful conversations with you, and just flat-out neglected you! *How would that cause you to feel?*

Men, you have to be able to put yourself in your "Special Lady's" position and ask yourself the tough questions about what she is feeling at any time when you act in a harsh or neglectful manner?

I am sure that you would agree with me that women are AWESOME! Most women have the truest and purest of intentions in their relationship with that chosen man, who happens to be YOU! **So, what happens in the process?** We STOPPED DOING the little simple things that truly matter to a woman!

We stopped elevating her to high above, and we stopped treating her like she is special or like she is a Princess! AND… none of these actions have anything to do with having to spend any money on her!

I am merely saying that we stopped delivering those powerful and intoxicating messages of love and caring directly into her heart! We are no longer romantic and caring in our approach to our Precious Lady! We no longer are being humorous and goofy when she needs it most! We stopped asking her about her day and what are her wants, dreams, desires, and goals!

We get lazy, sloppy, grumpy, irritable and sarcastic!

Furthermore, we progress to becoming harsh, rude and crude to our "Lovely Lady!" **Why does this happen?** Since you now have someone who you love and want at your side, we get comfortable and allow old, stand-by Dominant Mental Operating Programs to come to the surface of our conscious thoughts, and we begin to act out on them.

Pay Close Attention: You can turn it around, but you must first recognize the fact that you do have a severe problem. Once you do admit that you need to improve in this area of your life, then communicating with her gets more comfortable, but you must start accepting responsibility for your "negative-stinking thinking attitude."

"I only speak with words that build up my Lovely Lady."

Learning how to speak the secret language of love is hidden from view for so many men because they are too macho to think in such terms as love, kindness, thoughtfulness, and devotion! The macho and egotistical man believes that any man who would consider things like learning the secret language of love are a bunch of wimps!

Unfortunately, the macho attitude kind of man will continue down the path of mentally destroying many women through a constant stream of psychological warfare and emotional abuse! **BUT... NOT YOU!** Since you made a deliberate independent, conscientious decision to change and become a man that has a sincere and sensitive caring attitude towards his "Special Lady!"

Men, be sure to burn these philosophies into your heart and mind! These powerful self-improving attitudes are your new way and your new attitude! You can consider them as the primary fundamental building blocks of learning how to speak directly to your woman's heart!

Your Every Day Spoken Language to Your Precious is Love.

On the next page is an easy to understand review of what love is.

"I read inspiring positive-growth information every day."

Make this Your New Dominant Operating Mental Program

LOVE is patient. is kind. IT DOES NOT ENVY. IT DOES NOT BOAST. IT DOES NOT DISHONOR OTHERS. IT IS NOT { SELF-SEEKING, EASILY ANGERED } IT KEEPS NO RECORD OF WRONGS. LOVE DOES NOT DELIGHT IN EVIL BUT REJOICES WITH THE TRUTH. [IT] ALWAYS { PROTECTS, TRUSTS, HOPES, PERSEVERES } LOVE. NEVER. FAILS.

1 CORINTHIANS 13:4-8

Praise Her, Lift Her Up and Show Her Your Love Every Day

"It is my mission to be a man showing my Lovely Lady devotion and dedication."

Precept 1 - ALWAYS Lead With Love

I would say this is the number one action or behavior that you should adopt in your new man reformation process! To learn how to do this IS NOT hard because it is just a matter of you making an affirmative "CHOICE!" The Power of "**Choice**" is TOTALLY in YOUR control.

It is SOLELY YOUR responsibility to choose to be thoughtful, kind and considerate! Change your thoughts, and you will change your life! IMMEDIATELY!

"**Leading with Love**", means that the words out of your mouth are of love, kindness and a generous heart of patience! You now understand that **your words** are a reflection of your **thoughts**! Change your beliefs about your reality or the situation which you are in, and you automatically change the words that flow from your mouth!

Men, I say to you here and now, if you love your Special Lady and do not want to lose her, then CHANGE your thoughts on how and what you think about her. In a short amount of time, the words that you speak to her WILL change! It is up to you!

It is TOTALLY within YOUR control at every moment of your life!

Think of your lady as being the most precious love in your entire life. Think thoughts of how beautiful her spirit is. Think of how much she admires you and loves you!

In your relationship, you have the opportunity to build a love that is full of passion and devotion but first, you must now show the way, as a man who is aware and in control of himself within all circumstances.

Regardless, of what is taking place, you will "Lead with Love!" Your Special Lady will be blown away by your "New Attitude!"

She will be drawn to you because she most likely has NEVER met a man that is so self-aware and willing to change damaging actions and behaviors into such beautiful positive energy!

This single act of self-improvement is a powerful magnet for your lady. It quickly rebuilds trust and confidence in her mind regarding you! However, let's keep in mind that it may take some time with her believing because she must see with her own eyes that you are the "Real Deal" and that this is not some con game or a temporary thing coming from you. Be Loving and Patient!

"In all that I do with my Precious Lady, I will lead with love."

The "**Lead With Love**" principle is not what many women are accustomed to in their experiences with men. If you have been a miserable, mean and angry man, then at first, she may not believe that this is truly the real you that she is now experiencing. I tell you this so that you are mentally adjusted to this response of disbelief from her. No worries, for you just keep on growing in a "positive manner." She will come to KNOW that your new actions and behaviors are genuine!

Precept 2 - Love is ALWAYS " Kind, Patient, and Easy-Flowing."

Since you boldly and repeatedly state that you love your Precious Lady, then being kind and patient should be one of your patented trademark actions in the new and reformed you! This means that you are extremely slow to anger! Your mind should be Super-Consciously-Aware of your thoughts, feelings and micro-impulse changes that lead to irritability that comes out of nowhere. That being the case, you will find that as you practice making yourself Consciously Aware of what is going on in your head. You will develop the ability to disable negative energy **At the Speed of Your Thoughts** so that you maintain a peaceful and easy-flow.

This is all about training your mind in the direction that you want to go!

The words that you speak to your lady are ALWAYS gentle and easy-flowing, even when you are disturbed by other variables in life, including any mistakes that she may have made!

The words that you speak and your physical actions CLEARLY show what you think of your Precious Love lovingly. **Another mission of yours is to make sure that you convey love to your lady in a wide variety of circumstances in life.**

While it is true that sometimes life's struggles can pose a challenge to our mentality, nevertheless, you should be driven to rise above these obstacles and STILL convey your great love for her. Just remember in ALL situations in life whether they are good or bad, you still can direct your thoughts and actions in a positive manner.

You are now the Master of Your Thoughts.
You are no longer a slave to them!

"When I wake up in the morning I am full of life and love expressed to my lady."

You seek her out to give her much needed affection! She will never have to ask you again to hold her in your arms because you are now tuned-in and know that she needs to feel the power of your caring and abundant love.

You are working towards eliminating any kind of "non-verbal facial clues" or body posturing that would indicate that you are upset or irritable about anything!!

When waking up from sleep, you are ALWAYS aware of your attitude and ready to greet her with a smile and an easy-going spirit. Sometimes, your workday will not be so good, but you will still rise above it all and be kind to her!

This is because of all your new growth and personal development. You now can see that it is foolish and selfish to be mad at her for something that she had nothing to do with.

Precept 3 - Become a "Gentle- Easy Flowing Spirit" of a Man

Men, this does not mean that you are going to be soft or weak! Let's get real! Becoming gentle, easy-flowing, humble, understanding, empathetic and sensitive to her heart will ultimately mean that you are gaining strength. You are learning to share your heart and become more transparent and giving in the way that you boldly show your Lovely Lady a rich and powerful love.

Also, you are obliterating old negative tendencies and corrupted patterns of thoughts, actions, and behaviors that created negative energy within the relationship.

When you step into this realm of being, the people who matter the most in your life respect you tremendously. More positive energy surrounds you, and the Lady of Your Life can naturally become crazy about you once again!

The **Gentle-Easy Flowing Spirit Precept** is a life-long journey, but the first step is just learning how to be aware of your thoughts and actions, then going to work on modifying the worst ones first.

The Truth of the Matter is, if you decide to walk this path, then you will be making impressive gains eliminating the old destructive behavior patterns.

"As a New Man, I have immense self-control, and I always show love for my lady."

Again, this by no means will make you a wimp or a weaker man, but a stronger and more desirable man! **A "Real Man" Exemplifies COURAGE!**

Believe it, my friend; women do not want a man who acts like a selfish, belligerent and demoralizing bastard who sadistically crushes them emotionally! To determine if you are that kind of man, all you have to do is observe the behavior of your "Special Lady" for a few days, or weeks and you will have your answer!

If you find that you are one of those men who has crossed the line, and has caused her to be withdrawn or uneasy around you, <u>there is plenty of hope for correcting it IF you are willing to change!</u>

It is imperative that you are willing to make swift corrective, self-improvement within yourself!

The Bottom-line is this: Anything that tears-down your Special Lady MUST be flushed from your heart, mind, and spirit RIGHT NOW!

- *Do You Love Her? Do You Really Love Her?*

- *Do You Care About Her Emotional Health?*

- *Do You Want to Improve Your Relationship?*

- *Do You Want to Stop Being Known as a "Jerk"?*

Here is the deal: <u>Apply this Information, or the Relationship Will Die!</u>

You either start applying these tried, and true principles or your lady WILL BE GONE! Even worst, the relationship will go through a perpetual cycle of fighting, yelling, screaming, cursing and a barrage of blistering belittlement with the only outcome being shattered hearts and severe emotional trauma for the both of you!

"I am relaxed & easy during ANY high-stress event, yet tender and loving to my lady."

CHAPTER 15

Actions That Start Communicating to Her Heart

Throughout this entire study-guide book, I have been guiding you towards the primary objectives of improving your thoughts, actions, and behaviors. I've taught you how to communicate to your Lovely Lady's Heart.

To continue moving forward with more of your education on How to Be a Better Man, I have outlined seven "Proactives" for you to master during your transformative self-improvement journey.

Proactive Action #1 - The very first thing that you must do is to forgive yourself for your past blunders, errors, mistakes and any action that may have negatively impacted the fragility of your woman's love for you! Yep, you have blown it; but NOW, you must work on where you are at right now in the present. You have done stupid things, but now it is time to leave all of that in the past!

This is necessary because you do not want to be carrying out the recommended actions with a heart full of complete guilt!

The actions that you will begin to deploy are performed by you because you recognize how much of a negative force you have been in your Special Lady's world!

But no more! You are now building a new beautiful world around her!

I am a New Man and I Only Think and Act

New Man Mind Trainer # 17

I am a New Man and I only think and act with peace and kindness with _____. I see her as the Queen/Princess of my world. I will lift her up in my heart and praise her with the most beautiful words every day. I will greet her with goodness and abundant affection that warms her soul. My thoughts and my words spoken to her are always easy, gentle and understanding. Today as a New Man, I express my love to my lovely lady. My thoughts towards her are always positive, fresh and uplifting. I am a New Man. *(end of affirmation)*

"I rise to the challenge of making myself better every day."

Proactive Action #2 - Immediately go to **Chapter 12** and select one of the critical apologies that you would like to say to your lady. I want you to practice this apology until it flows from your lips with your heart, carefully woven into every word that you are to speak!

Remember, you were formerly one thoughtless and inconsiderate human being, so this is the time to consider all the damage that you have done so that once you present your apology, it has the feel of flowing from a heart of a man that is becoming a gentle, loving and easy-going.

Saying the Words, I am Sorry is Easy for Me

New Man Mind Trainer # 18

Saying the words, I'm sorry is easy for me. Whenever I say the words I am sorry, it comes TOTALLY from my heart. I am walking a new path and along the way in that walk, I am humble and sincere whenever I apologize. I deliver my apology directly into the eyes and heart of my beautiful lady. The words, I am sorry to my lady quickly heals and mends the mind and the heart. I am a stronger man and a better man because I now can apologize with an open heart when needed.   *(end of affirmation)*

Must Always Be Done with Intense Desire, Emotion, and Repetition.

I am Renewed in My Speech, My Thoughts

New Man Mind Trainer # 19

I am Renewed in my speech, my thoughts and my actions and it feels great. I am the only person responsible for the thoughts in my head and the words that I speak to the Love of My Life. I am a New Man, who strives to think and speak with words that heal and help. I easily speak to _____, with lovely, kind words that praise her and helps her to see I am her New Man. As a New Man, each day of my life I bring forth thoughts and actions that are good and full of joy for me and my awesome lady. I say it BOLDLY with unwavering belief and commitment, I am a New Man! It is heard whenever I speak, and my actions always support what I say.   *(end of affirmation)*

"My Precious Lady ONLY hears good, clean; healthy words flow from my mouth."

Proactive Action #3 - As mentioned in Chapter 12 – I suggested that you clean yourself up and be sharp! Yes, even when you are in non-work days scenarios! It is vital to understand that you are creating not only a new mindset for her but also for yourself and people who knew the *old you*. You are now in the process of becoming a "new man, " and even your dress MUST reflect this!

Scientifically, it is a proven fact that the way you look, and dress can have a significant impact on yourself as well as others! So, this action is critical in your new development!

Today is a New Day and I Present Myself as a New Man

New Man Mind Trainer # 19

Today is a New Day and I present myself as a New Man to _____, and to all who I interact with. My thoughts channel positive energy from the time I wake, until to the time I go to bed! My actions are strongly positive for my beautiful lady. When she sees me, I will look clean and ONLY good and healing words will flow from my mouth. I present to _____, a man that is confident and transparent about my feelings for her. My words spoken to my Lovely Lady causes her to smile, laugh and feel warmed to the inner part of her soul. I am positive. I am Kind. I am Gentle. I am Patient. I am loving. I am a New Being. I am a transformed man. EVERY DAY, I give to _____, awesome praise, kindness, gentleness and enriching love. *(end of affirmation)*

"I am a deeply caring man who is gentle and kind towards my Lovely Lady."

Even people who are familiar with you are moved to strong positive feelings and thoughts regarding you when they see the stout, clean-looking, sharp, nicely dressed person that you are becoming!

A Firm Warning! IF YOU FAIL to hold to form and slip back into your "old ways" with your lady, then that "new man" you are working to project, will be viewed as a "phony!"

Your Credibility Will Be Irreparably Damaged If You are a Phony!

Men, for those of you who are serious about becoming the man of your lady's dream: be ready to grow and do not play games!

Proactive Action #4 – Read books on love and communication. Listen to audio recordings of self-improvement, love and relationship development. Become a student of these kinds of materials. Throw out your porn and music that is negative, and degrading about people, life, and women! Get rid of all of that garbage IMMEDIATELY! I mean severely curtail the playboy magazines, porn website hopping, heavy Facebooking, extended cellphone time after work hours or anything that creates a distraction for your brain to generate healthy thoughts.

Garbage in = Garbage out! (G.I.G.O.) You are a by-product of all of this kind of crap that you have been pumping into your brain for all of these years!

Hopefully, you are now ready to make your "Special Lady" the number #1, for she is the most important human being in your life — this starts right now!

"This is a New Beginning for me - I bring a fresh, clean attitude to my learning."

> ### Burn this into Your Brain. FOREVER!
>
> The more that you are distracted with any kind of the listed materials above, as well as any other useless, mindless garbage, the more you increase your chances failing to redesign yourself, which in turn keeps you just the way you have been, which got you into the position that you are into today with your Precious Love. To become transformed in thought and action, and to become a better man, you MUST introduce to yourself new, mind-enriching, high-quality information on a consistent basis that eventually gives birth and fosters better thinking, which in turn leads to better actions, behaviors and habits. *End of Story.*

Through the Power of Choice, You CHOOSE how you want things to be!

Please revisit **Chapter 4** "**How we got so jacked-up**." You will be reminded of the reality of why you must make such a firm stand in this area of your life!

Initially, you formatted your brain for "Relationship Failure" with women.

Again, I emphasize that most of us are unaware of the influences that have shaped us and caused us to think and act as we do. However, the hope of today is that you have already begun the process of personal growth and change. Through a constant stream of new information, you can start to water-down the years of filth and the massive overload of mind pollution that has poisoned your brain, contaminated your thinking and led to your sometimes-undesirable behaviors!

Please, let the following permeate your mind; your thoughts are the cause of all of your habits, so whether it is a good habit or a bad habit, it is your thoughts that have shaped your life around you today!

The subconscious mind is the driving force behind all of our conscious thoughts, and it is what <u>directs</u> how we respond to the world around us! The vast majority of your conscious thinking (90%) originates from the subconscious mind.

"I fully enjoy learning on how to become a better, and it inspires me."

> "The good man out of the good treasure of his heart brings forth what is good, and the evil man out of the evil treasure brings forth what is evil; for his mouth speaks from that which fills his heart." Luke 6:45

What does this mean to you?

The subconscious mind does not know the difference between Truth versus Fiction. All the things that you say to yourself, or to someone else that is negative or hurtful, get absorbed by the subconscious mind. It DOES NOT know the difference between good, bad or indifferent! Overall, the corrupted information just gets processed and eventually works itself to the conscious level of thinking and being.

> The **"Dilution Factor"** or **"Neuro-Linguistic Programming (NLP)"** or **"Psycho-Cybernetics"** essentially all means the same thing. These are methods that utilize reading, verbally spoken words, statements, and audio listening to help change the way we think and modify behaviors.

Essentially, your brain can be compared to a computer software program. At present, your brain has a specific kind of software program or code on which it is operating.

Since you are the computer programmer of your brain, at any time, you CAN write a new software program code or script for your brain. Through the repeated introduction of fresh information into your brain via, articles, audios, videos and positive affirmations, you can begin the process of rewiring your brain! Thus, through direct and deliberate effort, you make yourself the Master Programmer of the New and Transformed You.

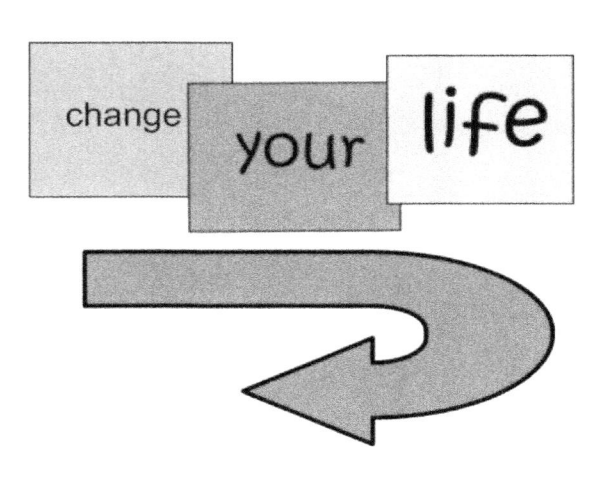

You can conscientiously determine precisely what you will allow into your brain. You can explicitly select the things that take you in the direction of growth, change and positivity for your relationship and rebuilding your future with the Love of Your Life.

"Daily I review my daily affirmations and healing takes place in my heart."

This new information will gradually water-down some of the powerful effects of the previous information that has been locked in your mind all this time.

Listen Up Bro! You must get rid of the old harmful and destructive habits in communication and relationship building. Say goodbye to them now!

The objective of such methods being applied to your self is to produce positive growth and changes that last over a long term! This is possible because we are "diluting out" the "old" with the "new." Though you never get rid of any of the old crap, it has less power over you because you are continually adding new positive information into your conscious mind, and it filters down to your subconscious mind eventually affecting the underlying construct of who you are.

How often should I practice and study these kinds of materials?

For the rest of your life!!! Becoming a "New Man" is a journey and you never arrive at the final destination. Striving for and reaching the higher levels of being a "Real Man" is an ongoing educational process throughout life.

It is very similar to following a lifetime fitness program. To get the best results, stick to the plan of being consistent and persistent.

Special Learning Tip! Personally, I like the idea of making my car a university on wheels, since I am in it so often. So, I listen to personal growth CDs & MP3s instead of the radio. I will tell you that I had the most significant breakthroughs with myself while driving my car and hearing new information as it is being absorbed by my mind.

Many men asked me the question, is all of this really necessary?

The answer is a resounding YES! It is **100% necessary** because you have to reformat your brain! You have to walk yourself willfully and joyfully through your own "brainwashing," to get the more highly desirable and impressive attributes of becoming a better man.

It is important to note that in life, most of us struggle with destructive vices, fragmented relationships, and poor communication skills. The way to improve upon it all is to make ourselves a better person. Generally, with the right knowledge applied, we can redesign ourselves and change the world around us. We only know what we know! Once we introduce a regular program of self-improvement, we not only improve the quality of life for ourselves, but for that "Special Lady" in our life.

"Every day I embrace new positive thoughts with passion and enthusiasm."

But, the bonus is that it spreads even further to others in your life, who see the revolution in your fantastic growth process. Overall, you become a positive example of personal growth to many people. You can now guide others through those dark, dismal treacherous waters that you once were lost and adrift in.

Proactive Action #5 – When speaking to your lady never swear or use foul language in your vocabulary. Also, never direct any negative inflammatory commentary towards her. Your lady is precious and very special. **Treat her as though she is the "Princess/Queen" of your world! Build her up! Adore her! Cherish her! DO NOT swear at her and curb your language around her.** Focus on your words, as you speak and become self-aware regarding your thoughts which is what drives your speech.

At first, when I attempted to stop cussing and swearing, it took me a few days to catch myself because my cursing and swearing had been going on since I was eight years old. I was an expert at it! Yeah, I know, it can seem like you are becoming a wimp as you get rid a lot of negative garbage in your behaviors, but again, keep in mind that you are training yourself. **You are becoming the Master and no longer the slave.** You CAN now express yourself with improved replaced thoughts, actions, and behaviors.

As you become a "Real Man" and are zoned in on becoming a better person overall, your words and the language that you "CHOOSE" to use is paramount to you being viewed as the "real deal."

F-bombs, blowing up all over the place, and cursing at your lady, children, parents and friends should be banned from your mouth, without exception! PERIOD! Quick making excuses and realize that you choose this behavior!

This again is usually another area of a person that must be worked on, because most likely, it is quite natural for you to rant, curse and swear when talking about issues of a highly sensitive or volatile matter.

Proactive Action #6 - STOP Abusing Alcohol and DRUGS! If you ever want to impress your "Special Lady" and start communicating to her heart, get rid of the booze and partying ways of your life! Your life should be dedicated to her! No, not solely, but enough to where she feels the power of your love and devotion to her, over all other things.

"I am driven with a loving heart to be a better man for my Precious Lady."

> **Developing new thoughts and healthy relationship patterns require that you become self-aware of your current thinking and behaviors. Growth and change takes work! To begin the process, it is strongly recommended that you regularly read books and articles 15-20 minutes per day. In addition, listen to self-help audios 5 days per week for 30 minutes per day. Whether you are reading a book or listening to an audio, more is always better.**

Many men think that drinking multiple beers every day is so cool! WRONG, BIG TIME! You are sliding down a slippery slope of alcoholism.

Though it may be true that you are not an alcoholic at this time, statistically speaking, the chances are high that you will be with continued regular use.

The buzz and the booze both are addictive! Your desire should be to find the most explosive and sensational high in life, and never let it go! This incredible rush of power can only be the love and devotion of your magnificent "Special Lady!"

The Power of the Love that you and your lady share, can be the most unmatched and thrilling non-stop high, ever imagined!

Men, Get This Into Your Head; Beer, drugs, and porn can NEVER take you higher, than the love that your "Special and Most Lovely Lady" gives to you, and the love that you should have for her!

The Love You Have for Each Other Can Take You Higher Than You Have Ever Been, and You Never Have to Come Down from the High of Such Incredible and Unprecedented Love!

Truth Be Told: You can find such power in your love, and it can propel you to become a better man than you are!

My Plea to You: I am sincerely encouraging you before it is too late, and you lose her! Throw away the vices or get the help you need, because just as surely as the sun will rise and set tomorrow. Your vices will eventually cause you both to lose!

Proactive Action #7 - Dump the stupid friends! **Grow a pair of extra-large-sized elephant testicles and be your own man!** Your lady will go crazy over you because she senses that you are becoming a bold, confident, independent thinker! She has heard that the nature of your conversations with your friends is changing, and she feels that you are now placing her before and above them!

"Clearly I see that my relationship with my lady MUST always be filled with love."

Positive Mind.
Positive Vibes.
Positive Life.

"Any negative thoughts within my mind, I instantly replace them with positive ones."

Let's Be Clear: Some of your friends will completely understand, and even seek out your wise counsel, on their relationship situation. However, there are others you will want to avoid or spend almost no time with! They are known as **"RK's" or Relationship Killers!**

These kinds of friends make it their mission is to continually get in between you and your lady with their words and a steady flow of negative commentary.

You can EASILY identify **RK's (relationship killers)** because they speak harshly or disrespectfully of your lady. They encourage you to do harmful, destructive acts that tend to cause heated arguments and problems in your relationship!

Trust me on this, these guys are TOTAL LOSERS! They know what they are doing by attempting to discourage you from personal growth and working things out with your beautiful and Precious Lady!

In my opinion, you should avoid them like the plague. Some of your closest friends may deliberately cause problems within your relationship because they are miserable with themselves. They may recognize that you have new-found courage that is making them uncomfortable with who they are. You now exemplify personal growth and development for becoming a better man in how you treat your Precious Lady. Secretly, they may be jealous of your new way of living.

As a "Real Man," you are going to step up to the plate and do the "right thing," as far as your lady is concerned! Part of your "job description" is to preserve the integrity and strength of the relationship! Make it impervious to the influences of the outside negative forces! Another part of your overall responsibility is never to allow anyone to ever degrade or speak negatively of your "Special Lady!" Additionally, it is your duty to make sure her name and honor are protected and upheld by you at all times, in ALL CIRCUMSTANCES! **How is this accomplished?** By being a "Real Man," and giving your "Special Lady" the complete love and devotion every day of your life!

"As a New Man, I always work hard to do what is right, fair and kind."

Special Chapter 15 Wrap Up!

I have just provided you with 7 of the most effective Proactive Action Steps that you can do to begin the process of communicating to your lady's heart, mind, and spirit!

Review Note: <u>The previously outlined 7 Proactive Action steps are all highly visible physical actions that are easily noticed when they are fully implemented!</u>

Imagine your woman quietly observing you in the delivery of these 7 Proactive Actions day after day! BELIEVE IT my friend, she gets it! She is becoming impressed with your actions. She is beginning to get moved and stirred at the central point of her soul because she sees her man growing, changing and becoming a "Great Man!"

If all good well, then in the very near future, your Precious Love begins boasting to all of her friends and even her mother about the reformation of your being!

You NEVER have to say to her that you are going to do anything because she can see it, hear it, and feel it in all that you are doing!

My friend, even right now as you read this information, your brain neurons are changing and aligning themselves for your transformation of becoming a new man. You just have to keep on with the growth and development action steps. The constant repetitive effort of your actions will stimulate the natural God-Given power of your brain causing it to realign, reassemble, redirect, redesign and rewire itself and bring forth a *New You*. Now that is something to get tremendously excited about!

Regarding the 7 Proactives outlined previously in this chapter in detail, follow this simple and most compelling rule down below in all human communication.

What you DO <u>speaks so loudly</u> that I cannot HEAR what you SAY!

"As a New Man, I always speak kindly to my lovely lady."

CHAPTER 16

A Better Way to Communicate... Do it!

No More Excuses!

We live in a fast-moving society today. Many people, for whatever reason, are unaware that the tone they use in everyday communication can come off as short, abrupt, rude, negative, condescending, snippy, demeaning and hurtful.

Seriously, are you paying attention to the tone that you use when speaking to your precious love? I am sorry bro, but I have lived it. I heard it for years! Sadly, most of us are tone-deaf to our own spoken words! We are totally out of touch with not only our tone but to what we are saying back to the other person.

Here is an excellent suggestion for healthy, non-inflammatory communication:

ALWAYS BE KIND When Speaking to the Love of Your Life!

- Be Consciously Aware of "**What**" You are Saying.
- Be Consciously Aware of "**How**" You are Saying It.

Question: Why do you use such irritability, hostility, and sharpness when you reply to the woman of whom you love so much? Sure, any of us could come with a litany of excuses to justify why on that day, or at that moment, we DECIDED to speak that way towards them.

The truth is, we deliberately CHOOSE to have a sharp edge at times when responding to our lady or anyone else. Yes, we CHOOSE!!! Every time! It is your brain and your mouth engaging with very little thought behind the action. So, if you claim you are unaware of this, then I strongly suggest that you pay attention to your tone and delivery.

Experts in communication suggest treating and speaking to everyone with respect and kindness. Be thoughtful of how we come across with our speech, non-verbal physical movements and facial gestures.

It is written: "**the words of the reckless pierce like swords, but the tongue of the wise brings healing.**" It is just one of many that I discovered in the Bible.

"I ALWAYS speak to my Precious Love with dignity and respect."

Think about your role or position in her life for a moment. The words you speak, what you say and how you say it deeply matters. All of this can carry a massive impact on the mentality of your Precious Lady because she has great love and respect for you. And, she hopes that you feel the same way about her as she feels about you.

When you answered their questions, or speak with a voice of frustration, it can quickly cut into her emotions negatively. You are a person in her world of whom she respects, admires and loves so dearly. This made it quite natural for you to be considered a person as a Highly Sensitive Role Model (HSRM) in her life. So, this automatically gives you heavy-duty added force and incredible power when speaking to her. And for you, she has a Highly Sensitive Role (HSR) to where she too must be careful of how she speaks to you.

Please refer back to **Chapter 4** for details on Highly Sensitive Role Models.

What is Up with the Sharp Wiseass Responses to a Question?

This is another major problem in human communication efforts, whether it be at home or work. There are far too many people, men and women, who instantly infect the other person's thoughts and feelings with negative energy, because of this "Wiseass Responder" type of communication. I used to be an expert at it but learned it was hurtful, thoughtless, ineffective and caused the set-up for an argument.

A snide, wiseass response to an innocently asked question is thoughtless and disrespectful to the person who is asking the question. And, if others are nearby and hear it, then they too learn quickly to be on guard with you. This kind of communication is now incomprehensible for me to ever do! It is flat-out wrong!

It seems to me that when a person asks you a question, it is an inquiry to gain insight or to learn. So, why be offensive and purposely create negative energy? **Why not just answer the question kindly with a smile?**

Now, some will say I was just joking around! Well, with the energy given to the receiver of your message, they like felt you were serious. They could not tell it was a joke from the way you said what you said. That is why it is best to answer kindly, directly and respectfully.

Honestly, when people respond in this manner to someone, it creates ill-feelings within the person on the receiving end piss-poor, garbage communication.

language and tone with _____ are easy, gentle and caring in ALL situations."

Useless and hurtful communication! Disrespectful and insensitive! When you speak to your lady this way, it is like they are your sworn mortal enemy to the death. It Is Harsh!

In life, plenty of people have innocent, non-threatening questions. Take a freakin chill pill and go easy on them. They are on your side and they care for you. You can easily hurt their feelings when you are being out of touch with how you are speaking to them. Learn how to pay attention to your mouth and contorted facial expressions that convey negative feelings or disapproving thoughts.

Wiseass speaking and short, sharp, abrupt responses and answers to an innocent receiver show thoughtlessness at work in your brain. It shows a lack of meaningful and caring thought. It shows that you may be looking to instigate and provoke evil intent. It shows that your brain is loaded with a desire to do emotional harm to the other person for NO REASON other than that is what you "feel" like.

Wiseass Responses = Dumbass Communications

Here's the sad truth; If you engage in this kind of conversation with ANYONE, then you have deep-rooted emotional issues that you need to rectify immediately.

There is no reason to be a quippy, condescending wiseass to ANYONE in your inner circle of family, friends and especially NEVER to the Love of Your Life.

Newsflash: Be Kind ---- At ALL Times!

Extend loving kindness in ALL of your words, actions, and deeds with your Precious Lady every day without fail. Work hard mentally to ALWAYS excel in this area of your life. Separate yourself from your old ways of thinking and being because you are a now a New Man of new mind and your mind surges with new thoughts that flow abundantly from your heart.

She is the Love of Your Life.

Be Her Man of Kindness, Love, and Respect.

"I only give goodness, kindness, and expressions of love to my Precious Lady."

Read Carefully: There is no need ever to be antagonistic or combative. There is no need to give responses to questions with a "Wiseass" tone or attitude.   NEVER!

Be the kind of man (person) that walks away from this insulting type of behavior.

It ONLY serves to undermine that quality of your communication almost every time. In the end, it only sets people up mentally to respond back to you in the same way. Trust me --- stay away from this kind of communication and your relationships will naturally be healthier.

When it comes to life, love and healthy communication at ALL Times with your Precious Lady, being a Wiseass... Makes you a Dumbass!

"I speak words that lift the spirit and the heart of my sweet loving lady."

Her questions can come about because:

- She did not understand the request you made
- She did not hear you clearly and want clarity
- She needed more information to get it right
- She wants to learn so that she can do it correctly
- She forgot the information and had to ask again
- She made an honest mistake and wanted to fix it
- She loves you and wants to know how you are
- You don't show her love, and she wants reassurance
- You are acting strangely, and she wants to know why
- You treat her poorly, and she wants you to stop

> None of this warrants being snippy towards another person at ANY time!
>
> **It is WRONG!**
> ⬇
> **Respond Kindly!**
> ⬇
> **At All Times!**

Listed above is a short list of 10 possible reasons your lady would ask you questions. None of them seem to be a good reason to get irritated or pissy and give one of those patented, useless, toxic and sharp wiseass replies! Good grief!

We all need some serious help from above because our spoken words are so full of twisted, spiteful and evil intent. With the bulk of that kind of destructive energy being spewed out onto the delicate emotions of the beautiful person that we consider to be the Love of Our Life.

Here's the deal: You are the one who is supposed to be in control of that mouth of yours. Act like it! <u>Another great idea is to slow down and LISTEN carefully to how you sound when you are speaking to your Precious Love</u>. If you want to be bold about it, ask others how do your comments and tone come across to them. If they happen to hear you speaking to her or others, then encourage them for honest feedback!

Being a Wiseass Responder is 100% counterproductive to the health of the self-image of those closest to you. It aggressively works against building meaningful relationship communication.

"My tone is ALWAYS gentle and easy when in conversation with my Beautiful Lady."

STOP! Let Yourself Be Guilty of this NO MORE!

To speak to another person, especially those closest to you with a "Wiseass Response" is thoughtless, and ineffective at creating positive feelings with the other person. When you CHOOSE to go down that road as a standard way of communication, you are setting up for a potential adverse reaction from those who are exposed to it.

We All Want to Be Spoken to with Healthy, Positive Words and Tones.

As an important side note; Pay close attention when your lady is speaking to you. Look at her directly when any communication is taking place, and do not allow yourself to become distracted by anything when moments like this come about! Take your cell phone and stuff it in your pocket. Give her the common decency of focusing on her, and the conversation at hand. These kinds of new actions show her that you care about her and what she has to say in a big way, as you should!

Lock these Down into Your Brain!

These kinds of deliberate conscientious actions speak loudly to her inner spirit, and she hears your actions saying the words, "*I am your man, and I deeply care.*"

- ☐ If you are asked a question, **keep in mind being a Wiseass does not favor a positive outcome because it is condescending and disrespectful on ALL levels!**

- ☐ If asked a question, answer fully with sincerity and kindness in your voice. In general, commenting with a nasty negative tone in your voice will often provoke someone to respond to you in the same manner.

- ☐ If she forgets something, there is no reason to scold her or berate her. My goodness! Be gentle. Be easy-going about it because we ALL forget. We all fail and fall short of the mark of perfection. Relax!

"My tone is ALWAYS peaceful and gentle when I answer any of _____, questions."

Here are a few sample questions with some of the poor responses that are somewhat typical for us to respond with. Just below the poor response, I present ideas for better answers that would serve to improve the quality of communication. The better responses show you are actively engaged and genuinely interested in her questions.

If asked: **"What would you like to eat for dinner or a meal?"**

Poor response: I don't know or whatever is fine.

Better response: Let's do _____ and some _____.

If asked: **"What would you like to watch on Television?"**

Poor response: I don't care, whatever.

Better response: Let's check out _____, tonight; sound good?

If asked: **"What color should I wear?"**

Poor response: Huh? Oh, I really don't care, whatever you want.

Better response: Oh, well you look great in both, but how about the _____.

If asked: **"What should I wear tonight or to a special event?"**

Poor response: Hell, I don't know! It doesn't matter, just do whatever.

Better response: I love it when you wear that beautiful black _____,

If asked: **"What would you like to do this weekend?"**

Poor response: I don't know. Nothing. Watch the game.

Better response: How about a movie, mini putt, go-carts and dinner.

Notice: The better responses are going to reflect an attitude of interests, which lets her know that you are listening to her. You can even go above and beyond the better responses and create other excellent answers!

Take from these examples to improve your communication with your Precious Lady, and show her that you care by your new attitude of being interested and involved in the conversation.

"I speak words that lift the spirit and the heart of my sweet loving lady."

Below are Two (2) New Man Mind Trainers Scripts. When you read and speak these scripts aloud, they cause you to become more <u>Consciously Aware</u> of your thoughts and actions. Repeating these Mental Brain Exercises (MBEs) also begin to create new and better ideas within your conscious mind, thus helping you to make better actions and eventually new habits that form the Transformed Man.

As a New Man, I Listen Carefully to the Questions

New Man Mind Trainer # 21

As a New Man, I listen carefully to the questions or thoughts verbalized by my lovely lady. I am attentive and engaged when speaking with my lady! I am involved with her plans for our activities together.

I answer all of _____, questions with kindness in my voice and I am always easy with the tone of my voice. Even though I may face other challenges in my day to day activities, when speaking with _____, I am calm and at peace. I am always relaxed and express to my Lovely Lady an easy-going man.

As a New Man, I give _____, my full attention whenever she asks for my input, even in the simplest of matters. I am committed to keeping all distractions away from our intimate moments and I am driven to stay focused on her. I am a man who steps up and eagerly show that I care about my Precious Lady's personal interests and randomly ask her details and questions regarding them.   *(end of affirmation)*

Must Always Be Done with Intense Desire, Emotion, and Repetition.

When answering any question from _____, I answer

New Man Mind Trainer # 22

When answering any question from _____, I answer her with positive and healthy words, statements and tones. My answers on whatever she asks, reflect a mindset of love, respect and admiration for my Beautiful Lady. And, because I am a New Man, I am mindful every day to praise and lift the heart of my Special Lady.

I speak with a fresh, upbeat attitude whenever we have our time together. I focus on the things she is sharing with me, and she can sense that my heart is soaring for her and that I care about anything that she brings to my attention.

My Special Lady is the Love the My Life and I speak words that build her up and let her know how awesome she is. I ONLY speak kind and endearing words to _____, even during times when things have been challenging for me or her. My heart is dedicated to all the facets of being a better man and treating her better than she has ever known or even imagined.   *(end of affirmation)*

"I listen attentively to the questions that my Lovely Lady ask and answer kindly."

Critical Instructions Before Implementing Chapter 17

> **Before utilizing the information in this Chapter you must be FULLY engaged in the processes of the 7 Proactive Actions in the previous chapter!**

There Are No Short Cuts! If you elect to by-pass the 7 Proactive Actions in Chapter 10, then you will fail in solidifying yourself as a "Real Man." The final result of this failure is that your Special Lady, her family and friends may determine that you are a fraud and a loser. (Ouch!) This could cause all of them NEVER to trust or believe in you again. You don't want to go there! So, let's get it right from the start!

- **Do Not Play Games with Your Woman's Heart!**
- **Be Ready to Grow and Become a "Real Man!"**
- **Study Hard, stay committed and apply the principles!**

You do not have to use the statements and words that are forthcoming in the next chapter. However, it is a good idea to memorize some of them and make them a part of the *New You.* These statements and words are designed to give you a starting point. You can build on them from there.

Practice, Drill and Rehearse them. Internalize the deep, rich meaning behind such statements, and learn to speak them with feeling from your heart!

You Can Make This Happen!

If you have come this far in your studies, then you are without a doubt committed to doing what is necessary to speak directly to your "Special Lady's" heart and be counted as the man she has been waiting for.

"I am energized to show myself as a New Man... not only in words but by my actions."

CHAPTER 17

Words & Actions Together, "Is Love's Secret Language"
Laser Beam Guided Precision to Your Woman's Heart

In the previous chapter you have learned what you MUST do to begin the process of communicating to your Special Lady's heart and redesigning who you are as a man.

It should be firmly evident to you that <u>your actions speak the loudest</u> when communicating virtually any message to anyone!

We as people understand physical action or inaction. In fact, it is the very reason that you are in this situation in the first place. Think about this. It was your actions that spoke the loudest, but the actions were negative actions that you heaped upon the most important person in your world! They were actions that caused her to lose faith in you, and have many people viewing you from a negative vantage point.

Your "new" actions **<u>are all proactive</u>**. They do not require you to announce anything to anyone about what you are going to do. In truth, it is usually best to keep your mouth closed about what you are doing, and **"just do it!"**

At this point, you are going to learn to combine your "new" actions with powerful statements, words and phrases.

Learn the powerful recovery statements beginning in the next 2 pages. These statements will help you to improve the quality of your thoughts and your communications with your beautiful lady.

"I will move my thoughts only in the direction of what is good and loving."

Remember when you were the man of her dreams?

> **Sign Up for Our How to Build a Better Relationship & Communication Blog!**
> A continuous source of **FREE** Informative Weekly tips, ideas, suggestions and solutions to assist you in personal growth and improving the quality of your relationship with that special someone!
> *** **Sign Up Here!** ***

⇩

http://blogsignup.howtobeabetterdude.com

She is waiting for "The Dream" and "The Man" to return!

Recovery, Renewing and Redesigning Statements

> Before you move forward with these "New Man Mind Trainer" scripts to begin healing your relationship and setting a new course for you and the Love of Your Life, I strongly recommend that you review them several times and embrace the full meaning of these statements until they start to become a part of you.
>
> Feel free to modify any words or statements that are more in line with the way that you speak and be natural at all times with your delivery.
>
> Visualize yourself going through the motion so that you are even more at ease and well prepared on any physical actions that you would like to introduce during your delivery.
>
> Bro, I am rootin' for you!

Are you close to your lady right now? If not, can you call her on the phone for two minutes? You only need a few minutes to let her know that you wanted to share some new ideas with her this evening that you learned recently. Even in this brief conversation, neither one of should be distracted. If that is not possible, then your initial statement regarding "your new ideas" will have to wait until she comes home.

The Setup: MUST BE with Absolutely No Distractions!

- No television!
- No computer!
- No children!
- No petting any animal!
- No cell phone calls! (turn them off)
- No cooking!
- **Psychologically, Be Ready to Spill Your Guts!**
- **Speak from Your Heart, NOT from your head!**
- **Always Lead With Love!**

"It is my mission to develop myself and be the best man that I can be."

[*Sit her down directly in front of you saying,*] "_____, please. I just need five minutes of your time with zero distractions! OR you can start with, "Hey My Love, can I have just five uninterrupted minutes of time with you to say something very important."

[*Then holding her hand and lightly stroking it, say to her…*] "First and foremost, I Love You! I am at a point in my life to where I clearly recognize and know that I have failed you and have done many things to wrong to you. In fact, I am now crushed by the pain that I have inflicted upon you. All this time, you have stood by me and instead of treating you like my best friend, I treated you like an enemy!

I have been blind, and nothing close to the kind of man that I should have been for you. Here, right now, what you need to know is that I am very sorry for being selfish, thoughtless, angry, mean and neglectful of you! Baby, I need you! I want you always at my side!

You and I together can make this work and, so I say to you IF at all possible, open your heart for me. Help guide me and show me the way. I am willing to learn and become the man that you need me to be! [*Kiss her lightly, on her cheek and whisper into her ear,*] "***I Love You and I thank God in heaven for being with you each day of my life!***" [*Stand her up, and just hold her!*]

This is the time to develop the real art of communication and learn how to share your heart entirely with the Love of Your Life! If this has to be done over the telephone, it can be just as effective, but you should be prepared for some odd moments of silence. Under these circumstances, be ready to fill in those moments with words, statements and phrases of how much she means to you, and WHY!

If you did end up doing this over the phone, I strongly suggest that once she does come home and is relaxed, do it again. Repeat your words and terms of endearment, but this time make sure you create a unique setting for your delivery.

* During this critical rebuilding phase of your communication with your lady **NEVER JUST TELL HER THAT YOU LOVE HER… TELL HER WHY!!**

From the deepest part of your heart, express what you love about her and how she causes you to feel regarding your love for her. Tell her with sincere, deep heartfelt emotion why she is so important to you.

"It is my mission to be a man showing my Lovely Lady devotion and dedication."

Setup #2: Over Dinner, whether out or at home. If you do this at home, you should make the dinner or order out for delivery. Quiet setting! **No Distractions!** You can either surprise her with dinner, or you can pre-plan it with her.

Caution: No more than two glasses of wine during the entire setting!

You have now been working in the realm of your **seven Proactives**. The changes in your behavior and way of being are being noticed. But remember you are humble. Do not puff up or allow your ego to create within you any false sense of accomplishment. This is because you still have lots of growth ahead of you.

Since your lady is now somewhat aware that you are acting differently, you can now spring this lovely, warm and delightful surprise on her.

[*Once you have dimmed the lights, lit the candles, seated her in her chair and have poured the wine. Say the following words or similar flow of context!*] **Speak from your heart and NOT your head!**

"_____, my whole life, I have waited for you. Once you were here, I failed to treat you like the Love of My Life! Much of what I have done shows that I have almost completely abandoned you! I have REPEATEDLY hurt and caused you great pain.

I have let you down countless times with empty promises of changing. I have cursed at you, and have called you the most horrible names out of anger and stupidity! I know those can never be used as excuses at any time since you are my most cherish and my precious love!

Yes, my love, you are my shining bright light of hope, and you are the warmth and radiant glow of love of my entire world.

So, here before you, and before God Almighty as my witness, I am asking that you forgive me for ALL OF MY thoughtless and selfish actions.

As a man, and hopefully, still your man, I am asking that you forgive me for ALL of the disrespectful and demeaning things I did that caused you rivers of tears, and days of quiet suffering. [*Let me be clear. This is not some game or anything to be taken lightly. You must be incredibly humble and sincere with every action taken and every word spoken. She must be able to see and hear that you are indeed a new man. Think of what she means to you and how much you want her always at your side.*]

"I am dedicated to healing our hearts & our relationship--- I will lead with love."

_____, please forgive me for ALL the times that I **ignored you,** and the **neglect** that I brought into your life.

What I am saying to you, is that **I am truly and profusely sorry for ALL of my actions and behaviors that I now know hurt you very much!**

I was IMMENSELY WRONG. I am working every day to be the man of your dreams, and become a man that you respect, adore and love with all of your heart.

_____, you are my dream come true, and I am nothing without you! You take me higher than I have ever been, and **I am madly and profoundly in love with you!** Just give me the words that you can and forgive me, and you will change my life for the better, forever!

I understand if you cannot forgive me at this time! It only means that I have much work ahead of me in earning your trust and confidence again! If that is the situation, I accept it because I am more than willing to do what is necessary to prove I am the man for you!

My heart, mind and soul are completely and immensely dedicated to having you at my side forever! _____, in case you have not heard me, I Love You! [*Stand up and walk over to where she is sitting and take your hand and lightly stroke her face. Now, lean over and ever so softly kiss her lips. Go back to your chair and sit. This is now the time for a real conversation to begin. You lead the way!*]

Be the Man Who Leads Your Relationship to Greatness!

"It is my mission to be a man showing my Lovely Lady devotion and dedication."

CHAPTER 18

Design Your Every Day

Of course, we cannot control all aspects of our day because many things happen unexpectedly and are totally out of our control. However, in designing your day, we are speaking in the sense of the things that you have direct control over, such as your thoughts, words, and actions.

When designing your day, it is essential to be aware that not everything will necessarily go as you envision in your mind. The intended purpose is to provide yourself with mental exercises to where you are <u>consciously giving your mind a roadmap or blueprint of instructions on how to perform for a multitude of circumstances and events that could unfold during your day</u>. You are providing critical information to yourself on how you see yourself as acting and reacting to the influences of those situations.

Visualize Your Day BEFORE Your Day Begins

Speak out loud and write down how you are to treat the Love of Your Life and all of those in your close circle of family and friends.

Imagine being a small passenger airline pilot. You as an airline pilot MUST ALWAYS do a "Pre-Flight Checklist" BEFORE you can even taxi down the runway! You have many lives that depend on you. Your skills to think clearly and communicate at optimum levels of effectiveness are crucial. You MUST also be able to fly safely in the worst of weather conditions and with the craziest of distractions. All of your training and repeated training are paramount to you being able to preserve the lives of everyone on board during the worst of times.

Your "Pre-Flight Checklist" MUST be done every time you are going to fly ANYWHERE. There are NO EXCEPTIONS! Well, in a similar way, the designing of your day involves a series of "Mental Walk-Throughs" and "what if" scenarios that could happen during your day.

"It is my mission to be a man who speaks with calm in the face of adversity."

This mental drill is to provide you with a roadmap or a vision for your day. You should write it down and build into it adjustments and course corrections in the event of unexpected turbulence during your day. This written plan indicates <u>what</u> you are going to do and <u>how</u> you are going to think and act as your day unfolds.

You are the pilot and navigator for at least two lives! You are bringing yourself and your Lovely Lady to a whole new spectacular place of love and happiness! It is your responsibility to navigate through this day and every day safely. You must strive to preserve your emotional balance, as well as all the people who you influence, contact and love.

Your thoughts, your words, your actions, your acts of kindness and goodness can inspire and lift people or send them crashing and burning! So, becoming a "Top Gun Pilot" is critical to your mission's success and the training that you receive is invaluable to creating a healthy and beautiful relationship.

Yes, you are the pilot and the navigator of how your day's journey will go!

You determine where it will go and how it will go. When you design your day, you deliberately and conscientiously "CHOOSE" to go forward into your day with a healthy positive mindset that is laser-beam focused on New Man Transformative thoughts and actions in all you do!

It is critical that you start your day by taking some time to envision your day. In other words, with crystal clear vision in your mind see how you want this day to go as you move through it. Embrace this vision allowing your emotions to feel the energy and imagery of this process.

Work Towards Becoming Totally Self-Aware. Since you are on this mission to self-improve and to develop new Dominant Mental Operating Programs and to transform yourself into a unique being, you want to channel your thoughts into seeing you, as this is a new person ALREADY!

This means that right now you are thinking, speaking and acting like this new person. See yourself as the very best you, who already made all the necessary adjustments that needed to be corrected, in thoughts, speech and actions.

Envision in your mind on HOW you see yourself interacting with people as you go out into this day.

"I am committed to expressing a heart of abundant love to my Lovely Lady."

How do you want to sound as you speak to people over the phone?

Is your tone positive and uplifting to all who you speak to?

Are your words anxious or stressed when you speak?

Do your tone and words help others with the challenges that they are facing?

How is your attitude in your day with people who you love, even when unexpected challenges and setbacks occur in your day?

See yourself applying the daily principles of reading for at least 15 minutes every day, speaking your affirmations, designing your day and listening to your New Man Mind Trainer audio.

In designing your day, you want to see in your mind that you bring the BEST possible *New You* to this day.

You now see yourself being Consciously Aware of your thoughts and if any negative thoughts enter your mind, **At the Speed of Your Thoughts,** you replace all negative those thoughts with positive ones.

Your new everyday actions are driven by a cheerful and kind heart because you have re-invented who you are. You can feel the once dormant seeds of greatness coming alive in you. You see yourself being calm and relaxed as you drive your car in the midst of rush hour traffic.

You see yourself at peace and finding simple solutions to solve ALL problems. You see yourself as no longer grumpy, irritated and moody, if those old feelings begin to rise, you snipe them out At the Speed of Your Thoughts and replace with them with thoughts and actions of calm, gentleness, patience, kindness, peace, love and laughter.

If something negative happens, you see yourself checking your feelings and emotions BEFORE you speak, instead of the old responses of anger and swearing. You instantly, **At the Speed of Thought, replace them** with clean, helpful speech. It provides fast, creative solutions springing forth into your mind.

"I am a better man because I have chosen to be so in the way I think and act."

Yes, in designing your day, you see yourself breaking the mental chains and shackles of the past! You know that you are no longer bound to the old ways, as you go forth in this day and every day.

This drill takes about three to five minutes to begin your day. Have a dedicated index card with about five affirmations written out sitting on your nightstand, and as you are preparing to get out of bed, grab them and read them to yourself and then speak them with the strong tone of emotion in your voice.

Special insight to encourage you...

I will tell you that due to the amount of personal growth and development that I needed, it would not seem possible that such mental exercises would have any impact of the kind of person that I was. However, the mental exercises and repetitive actions all started to work by breaking down the old me. The new me came to life in me and stayed on top. The new and improved Jeff continued to flourish because I remained consistent with my mental exercises and affirmations.

We ALL have the magnificent ability to rewire our brains and become more than what we ever knew was possible. **That is the way that God made us. He has given us the ability to think and re-direct our lives At the Speed of Our Thoughts!**

I promise you that if your desire is burning white-hot and you use strong, deep-rooted emotionality into your efforts, coupled with your affirmations, and continue to repeat this process, you WILL feel the power of change taking place inside of you at a phenomenal rate.

Designing your day is just one of protocols that I have outlined for you in this study-guide book. It is my deepest hope that you apply the strategy of designing your day in the way that you want it to go. This particular daily plan of action can accelerate the rewiring your brain, and it will excite you tremendously, once you experience the full power it.

Truly, the world around you will begin to change, and the Love of Your Life will experience the full power and beauty of a Transformed Man in her life creating a whole new world of passion, kindness and a beautiful, expressive love!

Remember, others may tell you that you cannot do it; but...,

I say to you, right now and boldly to your face, that YOU CAN!

"Every day I make myself self-aware of my thoughts and my spoken words."

You Are the Master Programmer of Your Mind

It should be overwhelmingly apparent to you that you are the ONLY ONE who determines what kind of information that will be going into your head.

Since you are creating for yourself a new set of Dominant Mental Operating Programs, you always want to choose information that builds you up and teaches you how to self-improve on your thoughts and actions.

In essence, you are in the process of becoming the VERY best that you can be in all situations and circumstances of work, play, life, and love. So, I am hopeful that you get intensely serious about this incredible transformation process of mind, heart, and spirit.

Truly, when you create a bright warming light of goodness around you, it is beautiful and attractive, and it can positively impact the world around you; whether it is your Lovely Lady or family and friends!

Special Note: please understand in all of this. We are still human and will have to deal with expected setbacks and things that mess us up. That's Life! None of us are perfect, so chill bro! Enjoy the journey and stay at ease and learn how to relax along the way. With that being said, I have found that the more you do these actions steps, the more often your days will go in the direction that you would like for it to go.

On a Personal Note: I pray and ask God to be my pilot in my day. I always have Him as my Great Counselor to help me through the tough stuff and get back on track.

Final Word: It is all up to you! The material you have in your possession DOES WORK! <u>How I am now, is the result of its steady application!</u> I am a transformed man. I am here to support you on your journey.

My friend, hear what I am saying to you…. The Love of Your Life is waiting for you to make this change. She needs for you to become a transformed man, so she can believe in you and trust you in all things!

If you want to save your relationship with your Heaven-Sent Gift, then it is ALL up to you. Just make the decision to be a better dude and treat your lady right by applying daily the lessons that are here in this life-changing study-guide book!

You CAN Do It!

I am rootin' for you!

Subscribe to Our Epic Blog for Becoming a Better Dude

http://blogsignup.howtobeabetterdude.com

"I am dedicated to healing our hearts & our relationship--- I will lead with love."

Your Personal Growth and Transformation Will Take Place IF You Have... Intense Desire, Along with Binding Strong Emotion into Your Mental Brain Exercises and Consistently Repeat the Process!

Men, I have provided you with the tools and information to assist you in a fantastic growth pattern for becoming a better man than you are!

Without a doubt, I know that if you consistently apply the principles and lessons of this study-guide book, you will be amazed at how much your lady will be moved by what she is hearing, and seeing, with your new way of being. It will be self-evident that you have transformed to become a "New and Improved Man!"

You may even be shocked to realize what she is feeling for you is a wave of high-energy emotions and heightened love for her man (YOU)!

If you hold to the Precepts, Philosophies and the 7 Proactives that are thoroughly outlined in this book, even YOU will be impressed at how awesome it feels to be a man that is no longer thoughtless and insensitive, but now kind, considerate and lives with a gentle spirit!

The journey that you have "chosen" to take by applying the information contained within this material will take you on the glorious new path to learning "How to Be a Better Dude and Treat Your Lady Right."

Get stuck or need a little help: drop me an e-mail and include your telephone number, so that I can contact you and see where I might be of service to you!

Jeff@HowToBeABetterDude.com

Subscribe to Our Epic Blog for Becoming a Better Dude
http://blogsignup.howtobeabetterdude.com

"I am dedicated to praising and lifting the heart of my Precious Lady every day."

Closing Words:

Decision and the Power to Choose

It is my greatest hope that you have decided to change and become the man that your woman believed in at some point in your relationship. Sadly, for some of you, it will be too late!

Although for some of you it may be too late, you can still take hold and rigorously apply the lessons from this study-guide book daily. You <u>can still</u> seek to improve yourself to be a better man for when you meet that next "Special Lady." You will already be ready for when the time is right for you meeting that next Special Lady of Your World.

We all have the power of "choice" in virtually all matters of our lives!

In life, so many of us fail to "choose" wisely with relationship decisions! The kicker in the whole matter is that we usually know when we were making a bad "choice." Sometimes it is just totally crazy the decisions that we do make in this area!

For me, there was a time to where I was totally jacked up in this area of life. I made lots of bad decisions due to my corrupt thinking patterns. So, I implore you to self-reflect and be honest with yourself, so that you can come forth and fully plug yourself into a process that can create magnificent personal growth for you and beautiful love in your relationship.

In closing, I say with the highest level of confidence that if you apply the principles, protocols, and procedures faithfully, you will experience a revolution from within. Your revolution will set you free of the chains, shackles, and burdens of the old corrupted mental operating programs of your past! Your personal revolution is the catalyst for incredible personal growth and development as a Transformed Man.

<u>And, that is the man who your Precious Lady is waiting for</u>.

Now, Go Forth in Your Power, and Make It Happen!

My hope is that she is still waiting for you to make the right decision.

"I totally enjoy learning on how to become a better, and it inspires me."

Brain Training Instructions

This simple routine will begin the process of building new Neural-Networks within your brain that gradually improves your thoughts, actions and behaviors.

Desire, Emotion, and Repetition are Paramount to Your Success.

- ☐ Read it to yourself 10-12 times per day for the next two days.
- ☐ On the third day, speak it outwardly multiple times throughout the day.
- ☐ Always Perform with Focus - No Distractions!
- ☐ Turn OFF the radio and put that damn cell phone down!
- ☐ Read two times as you awaken. BEFORE you get out of bed.
- ☐ Read two times during your morning coffee and/or morning work breaks.
- ☐ During the day make a quick phone call; tell your lady something loving.
- ☐ Send her a text or two to communicate words of endearment to her.
- ☐ Read a New Man script twice BEFORE walking in the door to greet your lady.
- ☐ Greet your lady with a warm, tender embrace when coming through the door.
- ☐ NEVER walk through the door on your cell phone. All attention directed to her!
- ☐ Read two times before you go to bed and contemplate the words spoken.
- ☐ Always read with intense feelings of emotion. Make yourself feel it deep!

Be energetic in your efforts to learn, grow, and implementation at all times!

Words of Caution: If you are lazy with your Mental Brain Exercises or your desire is lukewarm, YOU WILL FAIL to acquire the personal growth and development that is necessary for you to promote healing within yourself and your broken relationship.

I have found that the best way to approach this new experience of re-wiring your brain is to do so with an extreme enthusiast attitude. **Learning is enhanced when your emotions are heavily invested** in your actions. Make sure you have the "I CAN" mindset, and you WILL succeed.

It is also imperative to know that the more often you do these kinds of Mind Trainer Exercises, then the faster the new thoughts and creativity begin to become a part of the *New You*.

Train Your Mind in the Direction that You Want it to Go!

"Truly, I am a New Man. I Praise and Lift Up the Heart of My Precious Lady Every Day!"

Printed in Great Britain
by Amazon